THE NEW PAGANS

HANS HOLZER

THE
NEW PAGANS

DOUBLEDAY & COMPANY, INC.

GARDEN CITY, NEW YORK

CONTENTS

INTRODUCTION

"SEE PAGAN RITES IN FULL TECHNICOLOR," screamed the movie marquee at the innocent passerby. Pagan rites indeed! What the victim of subliminal and not so subliminal advertising saw inside the motion-picture house was nothing more than a lesson in anthropology: documentary films taken among the primitive tribes of New Guinea or Africa were being touted as something forbidden, exciting, and bound to get you all shook up!

The fact of the matter was that these rites were far from unusual for the people performing them, who do not view life by Western standards. But far more importantly, the primitive people of New Guinea and Africa are not pagans in the true sense of the word. The misuse of this term is somewhat similar to the abuse of the word "native." Everyone born someplace is a native of that country. Yet, when we speak of "natives," we often think of such people as being primitive or in need of colonial enlightenment. By the same token "pagan" means nothing more than coming "from the country." *Pagus* in Latin is a term applied to the provinces in general, as different from the cities. There are slight connotations of being somewhat more naïve in character, and a *paganus* is a "country cousin" by Roman standards of sophistication. But he is not a dolt or a primitive human being; he does not participate in weird rites or deny the blessings of culture and civilization.

Even in ancient Rome, the term *paganus* was not meant to be derisive, but merely to differentiate between city folk and country folk. In today's parlance, we have similar terms in the German and English languages. The German refers to a *gau* as an area which may have peculiarities of custom, likes and dislikes, geographical uniqueness, and in some way represent a small area within a larger context. In England, the term "district" is applied to a part of a county which has its own distinctive character. People from the district are generally people one knows better than strangers from afar. For those living in the same area, it denotes familiarity with each other and with the world in which one lives.

The exciting meaning of the word "pagan" as we understand it today must be blamed on the medieval Church. Christianity, as it entered Europe at the dawn of the Middle Ages, was at first an urban religion. The more sophisticated and perhaps even more civilized people of the town took more readily to the new faith than did the suspicious and stubborn country folk. For centuries Christianity was victorious in the cities and towns while it remained on the surface only in the countryside. Underneath that surface the old religion continued to exist and flourish. Priests would scorn these continuing habits of worshiping in the old ways, and referred to the people clinging to their old gods as pagan people. The term was, as I have pointed out, at first purely geographical. Country people still worshiped the old gods; city people no longer did, and therefore in the eyes of the Church were superior.

For several centuries Christianity and the old gods existed side by side. Other than to look down upon the multiple deities of the country folk, the priesthood did little to harass those who worshiped them either openly or underground. But when political conditions made it imperative for the Church to suppress all opposition, the term "pagan" took on a new and far more menacing meaning. You were either a Christian or you were a pagan; you couldn't be both. From this it was only a short step to deny anyone not worshiping in the Christian way the right to be a useful citizen. The persecution of pagans was clearly indicated if this was to be a Christian world, and Europe at the time of the Crusades was a Christian world indeed! The pagan gods were all devils, or demons, and those worshiping them evil per se. Gradually, not only those who could not bring themselves to accept Christianity were considered pagans, but even devotees of highly developed religions other than Christianity itself. Thus the pagans of the countryside found themselves strange bedfellows with such totally different religions as Islam, Buddhism, Veda, and Taoism. Only Judaism was in a class by itself, since Jesus had been born a Jew. Jews weren't pagans in the eyes of the medieval Church; they were far worse. They were, in fact, guilty of deicide.

Such an attitude toward pagan worship is based upon the notion that only the Christian approach to the deity is valid, and everyone else is wrong. It totally disregards the pre-Christian form of religion prevalent in Europe prior to the birth of Jesus, and paints a picture of spiritual wasteland existing prior to the arrival of the Messiah. Thus, medieval schoolchildren were taught that the Greeks and Romans—pagans all—really didn't get saved, but that in the end, with the arrival of Christianity under Constantine the Great, things turned out better and mankind finally saw the light—blissfully ignoring the fact that the Emperor Constantine took the Christian faith solely for political reasons to defeat his competitors for the crown, and himself was never actually baptized until the very moment of death. The Church in teaching history to the young did insist that Western civilization only came into its own with the arrival of Christianity as the state religion

For centuries this attitude toward religions other than Christianity was the only attitude one could safely have, for dissenters were severely punished. It was only toward the Age of Enlightenment, in the eighteenth century, that it was possible to discuss alternate routes to the deity. In prerevolutionary France, the idea of rustic life and its blessings first came out of the underground, where they had been pushed during all the centuries of Christian domination. The idea that life in harmony with nature was preferable to life in accordance with man-made religious doctrines took hold slowly, first among the literate and upper classes, who borrowed their ideas from the country folk of antiquity. The Renaissance had already unearthed many of the relics from the Greek and Roman past, showing their beauty and the great strides these ancient civilizations had made prior to the destructiveness of the Middle Ages, and now the spiritual blessings of living in tune with a pantheistic concept of nature were added to these discoveries.

After the holocaust of the French Revolution, the early-nineteenth-century romanticism again took up the cudgels for a rural life of tranquillity and meditation. Some of the writers of that time turned to paganism for their spiritual fountainhead. Even in the nineteenth century this was daring, for to confess not being a Christian had certain repercussions. These were no longer execution by a jealous Church, but social ostracism, and only a truly free artist could afford it. In the 1880's, various pagan lodges sprang up in Western Europe, emphasizing the ancient ideals of pantheism and worshiping the symbolic deities representing nature. Foremost among them were the Order of the Golden Dawn and the Rosicrucian revival movement based upon a seventeenth-century tradition of southeastern German origin. But these quasi-pagan movements did not replace Christianity entirely; rather did they accept Jesus as the great prophet, along with other great prophets of other ages, rejecting only the establishment of the Church.

The revival of paganism—or rather the return of pagan ideals—did not make very much headway during World Wars I and II. Preoccupation with material welfare, industrial and scientific progress beyond hopes, and a general orientation toward more tangible goals kept large masses from delving into the delights and advantages of the pagan life. But the 1950's and 1960's brought disillusionment with the various forms of Establishment government, Establishment religion, even Establishment philosophy. The young especially looked toward other paths to find themselves in their relationship to the deity. Parallel with the rising interest in the occult, a new wave of seekers after the pagan ways spread throughout the Western world. Not only a revival of an interest in witchcraft, or the Celtic form of "Old Religion," but other pagan cults of Mediterranean or Hebrew origin fascinate the young and those of nonconformist leanings among all age groups.

Nowadays it isn't necessary to hide one's desire to be a pagan, to call oneself a non-Christian. People do it and get away with it. They are not ostracized; they are simply looked upon as being different. Here and there, in some of the smaller communities where prejudice has always been strong against religions other than the majority faith, such people would be considered unacceptable to the majority of the community. But by and large it is possible to call oneself a pagan in the 1970's without being hounded by either Church authorities or the state.

The term "pagan" has taken on additional meanings. No longer does it represent the country folk and their unsophisticated ways; on the contrary, some very special people, highly sophisticated and frequently intellectuals, are the new pagans. A pagan, in today's terms, is simply a person who prefers to worship a multitude of gods or deities representing the various forces in nature. As we will discover further on in this work, pagans are also monotheistic in the sense that all gods are part of the One Force representative of the universe. The difference between a pagan worshiping a multitude of deities which are in turn part of a greater god, and the Roman Catholic revering the statues of saints who in turn are lesser representatives of the great Christian God, is really not so great as all that.

Where the basic difference lies, I think, is in the pantheistic concept of religion. To the pagan, nature is god. To the Christian, God is manifest first of all through his "only begotten son, Jesus," and from there in a descending hierarchy, through the popes, down to the priests, and ultimately the baptized individual. In the man-made hierarchy, there is no room for nature. In the nature-based pantheistic cult, there is no room for a man-made hierarchy. Even the pagan priest is only a channel, not a power.

The new pagans are by no means oddballs or students seeking to rebel against Establishment religion. They have as yet no articulate universal spokesman. Their leaders are barely emerging from the darkness of convention. Their publications are simple and circulate in small areas only. But they are in existence, aboveground, ever spreading to those who are ready to study them. Some of these publications are intellectually complicated and hard to obtain. *Protos* is published by the students of Los Angeles, California. *The Harp* is edited by Mark Roberts in Dallas, Texas. And in London, Douglas M. Baker, M.D., a member of the College of Surgeons, is the editor of *Aquarius, Journal of the New Age*. In a recent article in the *Saturday Review* entitled "Visions of a New Religion" by Marcia Cavell, the author looks at the emerging new cults as a sure sign of the coming change in man's spiritual relationships with the deity principle. She sees the political reformers ultimately veering toward a new religious concept, and a new kind of reality. "It will reunite what we say with what we think and do, feeling with thought, unreason with reason, mind with body, us with ourselves and each other. It will join us in genuine community. There will no longer be rumors of angels (to borrow a phrase from Peter Berger), for they will be among us and we shall be they."

I have personally examined the current state of the various neopagan movements, by listening to their teachings, involving myself with their rites, and trying to understand them not as a casually interested outsider but as a truly uncommitted and open-minded friend. In the process of this work, my own pantheistic leanings have become more pronounced, but I find this no hindrance in evaluating that which I have experienced, seen, and heard. One can be a pantheist and yet remain true to those portions of Christianity that are the very essence of Christ's teachings. Ultimately, all paths to truth merge in the distance. Perhaps I can make this distance a little shorter through these pages.

The material for this work had to be sifted, organized, and frequently condensed. Some of it could not be published for a variety of reasons—chiefly the need to respect the expressed desires of those who have confided in me as to secrecy of certain rituals. I have been permitted to publish far more than anyone else has ever been able to of pagan rites, incantations, rituals, and beliefs, and if the reader progresses to the point where that which I have published is insufficient and that which I have kept secret is desired or required, then he will also find the way to seek those who can personally and individually dispense that ultimate knowledge he seeks.

THE NEW PAGANS

BOOK ONE

THE HEIRS OF WICCA

Solemnly the tall young man raised his dagger toward the window. There were five of us seated around a low table in a semi-dark room above a Manhattan nightclub. Outside, the busy evening traffic of the West Forties created an incongruous background of worldliness, technology, and people going places to spend an evening of fun. Here, in this cold room above the nightclub, a witches' circle was about to be cast and consecrated. The doors had been locked, shades drawn across the window, and the only light in the room came from two flickering candles.

Terry, a twenty-six-year-old telephone company employee, had risen from his chair, half mumbling the first words of the incantation. "I conjure thee, O circle of power, that thou art the boundary between the world we knew and the realms of the mighty ones, the guardian protection that shall preserve and retain the power which we shall raise within thee. Therefore I do bless and consecrate thee. I summon, stir, and call thee up, O mighty one of the east, to witness our rites and guard our circle." Facing toward the east, Terry then drew a pentagram in the air, using his athame, or sacred dagger. Facing south, he repeated the incantation, inviting the mighty one of the south to join the circle. Again drawing a pentagram in the air, he proceeded west and then north, until the four "lords of the watchtowers," as some witches call them, had been properly summoned and presumably were present at the ritual.

I had brought a bottle of wine to serve both ritually and socially. One of the young ladies who had come with Terry reminded him that he ought to bless the wine prior to opening the bottle.

"Right," Terry nodded, and proceeded to lift the bottle toward the east, saying at the same time, "I exorcise thee, O creature of wine, that there may be cast out from you all impurities or uncleanliness of the spirit of the world." With that, the bottle was opened and Terry sat down again.

This wasn't going to be a big ritual, to be sure. It was a first meeting of what might turn into Manhattan's newest coven of witches. To begin with, we hadn't properly prepared for the entire ritual. Although I had spoken to Terry many times before, this was the first occasion when we met face to face. Witchcraft is an intimate religion. It is best that those who will worship together also get to know each other well before they proceed to the rite itself. With Terry were two young ladies who wanted to see what witchcraft was all about, and with me was a young woman who had read *The Truth About Witchcraft* and was inclined to become a witch if someone would initiate her. We all wore street clothing, and only Terry and I had brought the witchcraft daggers a witch is expected to own. Mine is a fourteenth-century Italian dagger which I had acquired in Paris during my antique-hunting expeditions. I had always thought that if I were to attend a witchcraft rite, I might as well be properly prepared. London high priest Alex Sanders himself had blessed my dagger for me a few months before, and the white ivory handle and darkly encrusted blade drew admiring glances from Terry and the others as I placed the athame upon the table.

The two secretaries Terry had brought with him watched the

proceedings in awe. One of them was his fiancée, and it seemed to me that she was not about to become a witch. However, she eyed Terry with adoring glances, and, knowing the power of a woman in love, I began to wonder whether Terry's days as high priest might not also be limited. He had recently left a Brooklyn coven to strike out on his own. What he had learned stood him in good stead, for the high priestess with whom he had briefly shared the honors in Brooklyn is a learned young lady. But Mary Nesnick and Terry had what are best called "doctrinal differences," and the parting was entirely amicable, as partings in witchcraft usually are.

Since this was a first meeting with the possible intention of forming a new coven, the discussion turned to the reason why these people wanted to be witches. Terry himself had only been initiated that same year; prior to his entry into witchcraft he had been a Roman Catholic.

"All the religions are the same thing to me," he explained, "but the Craft to me relates to happenings in the everyday world much better. When you see somebody being hurt, you can understand why. When you sit there and feel the seasons come and go, you can go out in the woods and feel it. The Catholic Church doesn't teach me anything about the seasons. When I stand there and feel the leaves falling, I actually feel the whole earth dying. I feel the grass in the springtime coming up. I can relate to this much better through witchcraft than as a Catholic. The pagan faith is more related to the universe. The Church doesn't teach you anything about that. You feel that your destiny is all made up between this man who is trying to get your soul, and another man who is trying to win it from him."

"Is the ceremony an emotional experience for you, as well as an intellectual one?" I interjected.

"That is hard to define," Terry answered, "because they are like two circles overlapping each other. You can't really relate to them unless they are both together. One without the other is absolutely useless. If you don't take care of the body, you're not going to be able to take care of the spirit. There has to be a balance. Some people think that Wicca is an erotic religion. It may be erotic, because some very puritanical people might think that it is. During the initiation there is a certain amount of kissing, and parts of the body touched."

"You know, of course," I reminded Terry, "that there are certain rituals in Wicca where sexual intercourse does take place."

"Yes," Terry acknowledged, "but this only takes place between either two lovers or two married people. As for myself, I have nothing against it. There is the Great Rite used in initiations of the third degree. The Great Rite means making ritual love, but witches don't believe that sex is the only thing. They find it enjoyable, and it helps the mind develop intellectually and emotionally. In moderation and at the right time, this sort of thing can be very beautiful."

"Doesn't it depend on the individual coven, and their own personal attitudes toward greater freedom in sexual matters?" I asked. It wasn't that I needed this information from Terry, but I was here to learn how he, as the priest of a new coven, felt about this matter. What I might have learned elsewhere was of lesser importance.

Terry hesitated somewhat to answer. "When I was initiated into the third degree and made a high priest," he finally explained, "we did not go through the Great Rite. There may be personal reasons or perhaps this is the priestess's particular brand of modern Wicca. At any rate, I do not necessarily agree with her." Evidently, Terry had an open mind concerning the performance of the Great Rite. "Sex is out of context to Christians, especially to puritans," he said. "This is the attitude of St. Paul, who never married and who I think was very anti-woman. That is why there are no women priests in Christianity. Among Jews, there are similar attitudes, but in the Anglo-Saxon and Celtic world, woman has preference over man. Here the priestess is above the priest because the Mother Goddess, represented by the priestess, is the one without whom the community could not exist. Wicca is the only religion of all religions with a female deity and a female orientation. Therefore it is a religion of love. Other religions, especially Christianity, are male-oriented, and they are religions of power."

I decided to question the two young girls who had come with Terry as to their attitudes toward paganism and possible interest in witchcraft. Both Jean and Barbara knew only that they wanted something different from what they had, but weren't at all sure that witchcraft was the answer. They had come because they knew Terry and were impressed with his views. Terry explained that he was going to start a new coven, but he had a special problem in that his fiancée was not about to become his high priestess, and what is a high priest without a priestess? And if Terry was to work with an outsider, how would his fiancée feel about it? One look at the girl's eyes gave me the answer: she wouldn't like it!

The conversation turned toward the practices of Alex Sanders, head of a London coven of which I have written extensively in *The Truth About Witchcraft*. Someone remarked that Sanders initiated only married couples. Both Terry and I shook our heads. In Wicca any consenting couple who had had the hand-fasting ceremony performed are "married." They are not necessarily married forever, but for as long as they wish to stay together. This is not a legal marriage as the term is usually understood, but it does mean that when two people stand before the high priest and at that moment wish to be united, he may not question them about it. It is true that Sanders will initiate such pairs only into the third degree of witchcraft. But that means merely that he will not take on strangers or outsiders. If two people come to him together, as a unit, even though they might have met five minutes before, he will take them through the rites as one single person.

"My fiancée wouldn't have to be bothered with the circle

at all for me to operate as high priest," Terry explained. "There is no reason to. There are certain occasions when traditionally you make love, such as on Hallowe'en, when the Great Rite is performed, or when you bring a single person up to the third degree. If it's a man, he has relations with the high priestess, and if it's a woman, with the high priest. But this can be done symbolically, and even if it is not done symbolically she wouldn't be there. If I come back to her, she knows I love her. But if it would hurt her I would rather step down as high priest. I want to be a high priest, and I want to have a coven. My fiancée could be present at many of the rites; there is nothing in the Book of Shadows against it. If she were to be my wife and yet not practicing as a witch, it would not mean that she isn't working with the community."

"How many people do you have at present who are interested in forming this group with you?" I asked.

"Well, there's Barbara here, and Aldo, and there is another person who works with me. Various other people have asked me about this group, but I let them ask me a few times to make sure they are a little more than just curious before I bring them into the fold."

There was also Ingrid, a model whom Terry had picked as his future high priestess. To make things a little more complicated, Ingrid apparently had a boy friend, and Terry, of course, was engaged.

The meeting broke up around midnight. To the young lady I had brought, it seemed rather tame. Perhaps she had expected everybody to take his clothes off and plunge head on into a heavy ritual. But witches go slow, and are generally suspicious of strangers. They want to make sure that the motivations for joining are right, and right motivations must include spiritual unfoldment as well as the desire to be in tune with nature.

During the weeks that followed I had many conversations with Terry. We compared notes on the Book of Shadows he used and the ones in my private library. By and large, witches' covens use similar rituals and similar wordings, but the exact text does frequently differ. The general meaning is usually the same. Since the Book of Shadows is always copied in longhand from someone else's Book of Shadows, those rushing to the nearest public library and asking for one are in for a disappointment. No one but a bona fide initiate of a coven should own a Book of Shadows. But parts of such books have recently been published, by me for instance in *The Truth About Witchcraft*, and also by Alex Sanders himself. With Terry's permission, here are some excerpts from his Book of Shadows—not enough to make you, dear reader, into a witch, but enough perhaps to stimulate your interest in the Old Religion.

A cauldron rite for the winter solstice. "Place the cauldron in the south; wreathe it with holly or ivy. Light a fire within making sure there is no light but the candle. Draw down the moon [a specific ritual open to initiates only] while the high priestess stands behind the cauldron, symbolizing the rebirth of the sun. The high priest should stand facing her with a candle and the Book of Shadows. If necessary an elder may aid him. The others move slowly around and each lights a candle from the high priest, who has lit his from the cauldron. Then the incantation is read. After this the 'five-fold kiss' is given by all males to the high priestess."

One of the great holidays of witchcraft is All Hallows' Eve, commonly called Hallowe'en. Essentially a somber and serious day commemorating fall, the resurrection of the dead to a new life, and the changeover from the reign of the high priestess to the reign of the high priest for the following six months, this festival has nothing to do with the common image of Hallowe'en high jinks. I have already described the rites in some detail in my previous book dealing with witchcraft. Here are some marginal notes from Terry's Book of Shadows, concerning Hallows' Eve. I have been permitted to quote short passages only; the rest is for the initiate to discover for himself.

"Walk or slow dance with candles. The high priestess evokes

the god with her athame, preceded by the 'witches' rune.' [This is a chant. I have published one of the witches' runes in *The Truth About Witchcraft*.]

"After the rite, all females give the high priest a five-fold salute, and again all females, as the high priest should be thrice consecrated. Cakes and wine, dance and games, if possible afterwards. And if possible, the Great Rite."

Also contained in this particular Book of Shadows are the "eight paths of realization." These are: 1) dance and similar practices; 2) wine, incense, drugs, whatever is used to release the spirit but be very careful; 3) meditation and concentration—this is the practice of forming a mental image of what is desired; 4) rites, charms, spells, and runes; 5) scourging with the scourge, a symbolic ritual; 6) control of breathing and blood circulation, and similar practices; 7) the Great Rite, described previously; 8) trance, astral projection, and other psychic practices. "These be the eight ways of magic. You may combine many of them into one experiment, the more the better. The most important thing is one's intentions. You must know you can and will succeed. This is central in every operation. Remember, you must be properly prepared according to the rules of the Wicca. Otherwise you will never succeed. The circle must be properly purified. You all must be purified several times if necessary, and the purification should be repeated several times during the rites. You must have properly consecrated tools, and all doors should be locked securely so there is no thought of interruption. Your mind must be clear of fear of discovery."

The best known of the witch's tools is the athame, or sometimes a sword. The athame, or short dagger, is never used for killing or cutting, but merely serves as a ceremonial tool. We are not told how the original athame was consecrated, but a newly initiated witch must have his or her athame properly sanctified. The easiest way to accomplish this is to transfer power from an already consecrated tool belonging to another witch. The instructions for this process are very explicit. Here is part of what the Book of Shadows says concerning the consecration of an athame.

"If possible, lay any weapon touching an already consecrated one: sword to sword, athame to athame. Cast the circle and purify as usual, keeping in mind that all tools must be consecrated by man and woman, both as naked as drawn swords. Place the sword or athame on the altar, saying, I conjure thee, O sword or athame of steel, that thou serve me for strength and defense, in all magical operations against all my enemies, visible or invisible, in the name of —— ——. [I am not permitted to disclose here the actual names of the god and goddess. These names vary from coven to coven, and many are known to me privately. Only the initiate will learn what the particular god's and goddess's names are when the time comes.]

"I conjure thee anew by the holy name —— —— that thou securest me for a protection in all adversities. So said me. [At this point, the tool is sprinkled and censed; then the conjuration continues.]

"I conjure thee, O sword or athame of steel, by the Great God and the Gentle Goddess, by the virtue of the sun, of the stars, of the spirit who presides over them that thou mayest receive such virtues that I may obtain the end that I desire in all things wherein I shall use thee by the power of —— —— ——.

"Now the owner of the tool about to be consecrated salutes the high priestess and the high priest by drawing in the air the appropriate symbol of their office—that is to say, conforming to the degree which either one of these officers holds in the coven. Then the new tool is placed between the breasts, and the two workers' bodies should then embrace, it being held in place by their bodies. The tool should immediately be put into use." Lesser tools are the wand, candles, and vessels for water and oil, the chalice, the scourge, and the cord.

While I was waiting for the next meeting of the coven to be called, I heard again from Terry. Whether the difficulty of working with both a nonwitch fiancée and a priestess at his side

was too much for him to resolve at this time, or whether he
simply felt the need for additional instruction, he had decided
to join Ray Buckland's Long Island group for additional work.
Ray had received him courteously and encouraged his further
studies under his guidance. This was particularly gratifying since
Mr. Buckland is somewhat choosy about whom he admits to
his proceedings. The Buckland Museum of Witchcraft and
Magick is located in Brentwood, Long Island, and Ray Buckland is the author of a number of instructive booklets dealing
with the craft.

Perhaps the surest sign that witchcraft is a bona fide religion
can be seen in the fact that each coven believes it is closer to
the truth and anyone from a different coven not quite as enlightened or trustworthy. In time, perhaps, this attitude will
change and all pagans will recognize each other as members
of one and the same family, the human race.

*

Five people, reasonable, gainfully employed, no special hangups, meet above a nightclub in mid-Manhattan to discuss
witchcraft. A new coven is about to be formed. The date is
December 1970, not the Middle Ages, not even the terrible
times of seventeenth-century Salem, Massachusetts. The secrecy
of the meeting is self-imposed. I am sure the nightclub owner
downstairs couldn't care less, as long as the people who rented
his upstairs for a couple of hours behaved well and didn't
attract attention. Similar gatherings surely are taking place all
over the country. The pagan revival is on the march. Most
colorful and attractive of all the pagan cults and religions seems
to be Wicca, commonly called witchcraft. To some, the term
is an unfortunate misnomer, creating the image of an old hag
riding through the sky on a broomstick. To others, it has
mysterious and promising overtones. Either way, it is a powerful
word.

Today, more people are interested in learning about witchcraft than ever before: not because Christianity, Judaism, or the other great religions have failed them, but because they seek something more vital, more personal, in their lives than the orthodox faith can give them. Witchcraft is a very basic religion, accepting all initiates as equals before the altar, dispensing with dogma and hierarchy in favor of individual links with the deity through sensual and extrasensory release. Small wonder that the Establishment churches fought the Craft, for witchcraft is nonpolitical, nonpatriotic and not of this world. It is a pantheistic faith in the purest sense, under which nature, man, and god are truly as One.

As long as man is able to think, reason, and feel, he strives for a better life and reaches up to the heavens to pull down some of the blessings of nature denied him before. If magic is a way to obtain these benefits, then he must apply magic and the rituals making it work. He does this without the stigma of original sin, false guilt, or blind dependence on man-made law; truly free, he is led only by his conscience, and as he practices the Old Religion in a new age concept, he restores to the word "religion" its original meaning, long lost in history: a link with God through nature.

Those most intrigued by the mysteries of witchcraft are the young and women of many ages: the young, especially those in rebellion against the established forces in the world, see in witchcraft a religion their elders can't share; they relish the special position that being witches will give them in the community. The current musical idiom, with its accompanying drug habits, is not so different from the frantic chanting and dancing of the Sabbath, and the unguent with which witches of old used to anoint themselves for an imaginary trip to the Blocksberg is the direct precursor of LSD. Witches of old brightened their drab lives with the monthly joys of the community rite, the esbat; young rebels of today, from militants and protesters to hippies, let their long hair down in a cacophony of abandonment to sound, sight, and scent.

Witchcraft is a female-oriented religion, while all others are male-dominated, relegating women to secondary or even minor positions within the faith. The high priestess is truly at the heart of the coven; her role appeals to the emotional, intuitive element in women, who flock to the Old Religion in increasing numbers.

Witchcraft had its origin at the very dawn of mankind, long, long before there were Christians and Buddhists and even Hindus, old as these faiths are. In the Stone Age, mankind's time was divided between hunting, fishing, and fighting on the one hand, and the domestic pursuits of agriculture, homemaking, medicine, and maintaining the fire in the hearth on the other. The hunting, fishing, and fighting were the jobs of the man, the rest the domain of woman. Life was possible only if one came to terms with the forces of nature, be they terrible or friendly, and so these forces were worshiped as deities by the simple people of the Stone Age. Presiding over all hunting activities was, of course, the horned god of the hunt. Men would impersonate this deity by wearing animal skins and horns in dance rituals called *sympathetic magic*, believing that dressing the part makes one into the character one represents. From this costume, the Christian Church of the Middle Ages constructed the fantasy image of "the horned devil."

Women, on the other hand, had the dual task of propagating the race through fertility and of maintaining the home as guardians of the fire, so the Mother Goddess was naturally female. Woman's place in primitive society was more important than man's, and so the old horned god became subordinated to the image of the Mother Goddess.

In worshiping the sun, the Stone Age people thought of the male god of the hunt, while the moon, the night, and all the mysteries of life were associated with the Mother Goddess. Every civilization had a religion of this kind: in Western Europe it was simply the horned god and the Mother Goddess; in Greece, Pan and Diana; and in Asia, Cybele and Atys. As time went on, the priestess of the Mother Goddess added medicine and a knowledge of nature's herbs to her storehouse of knowledge. The question of life and death was always important in primitive society, so communication with the dead also mattered and again the priestess was in charge. Only during the winter season, when the hunter was in his element, did the male priest preside at the religious gatherings, and primarily in a ceremonial function. The word "witch" itself means merely Wise One.

The Old Religion, as it was called when Christianity appeared upon the scene, coexisted at first peacefully with the new faith. In fact, early Christianity borrowed much from the older religion, incorporating native customs, raising churches upon sacred pagan sites, and allowing the country people to continue going to the witchcraft gatherings, the Sabbaths, and the esbats, so long as they also came to church on Sunday.

But by the seventh century, Christianity had become a fanatical religion, and the continued influence of another religion side by side with the Church became troublesome. Added to this threat was the beginning development of reform movements. By the tenth century, such sects as the Albigenses and Waldenses had risen and were ruthlessly exterminated by the Roman Church.

The Old Religion felt that the climate of tolerance had changed and went underground. But despite a decline in the number of its people, there was continuance of worship in Western Europe all the way from the Stone Age to the present.

The Church had turned the gods of the pagans into demons. Every evil, every disease, quite naturally was the work of some specific demon who had to be discovered and destroyed; as yet, the devil had not been born. The peasant war of 1364 showed the Church how dangerous the organized discontent of the underprivileged masses could be, and a scapegoat had to be found. Some Church theoreticians thought of creating a central figure who would be the feared Antichrist, the counterplayer whose presence in this world was the cause of all evil, and who, conversely, was kept in power only because of the sins committed by some men. At the head of the list of such sins was the sin of not accepting Church dogma and Jesus Christ as the Son of God. The practitioners of the Old Religion, having worshiped their way without Jesus for so long, quite naturally saw no reason to submit to such a philosophy.

But the Church was not satisfied with the figure of a vague Antichrist; he took shape in the identity of the horned devil, conjured up as a mixture of the ancient Phoenician deity Beelzebub, Pan, and the horned god of the hunt, and nurtured by the fertile imagination of a sexually and intellectually frustrated clergy who were forbidden any form of discussion or even constructive thinking outside Catholic doctrine.

Torture, punishment for one's sins, and physical suffering were part of medieval thinking, and so the devil visited all those things upon the poor souls he managed to snatch. Witches, the Church asserted, had a compact with the devil and therefore were his associates. By 1485, the Pope had been persuaded to persecute them actively en masse, and from then on hundreds of thousands of innocent people died in the most horrible ways. The two great waves of witch-hunting, from the fifteenth to the seventeenth centuries and again in the late seventeenth century, when the Puritans equaled their Roman Catholic brethren in ferocity, were a carnival of death sparing neither high nor low. Accusation of witchcraft was tantamount to conviction, and many were caught up in this madness simply because a neighbor wanted their property badly enough to accuse them before the authorities. The belief in the devil was so universal that anyone stating he didn't exist would automatically convict himself. Witches do not believe in the devil, but in a happy life free of sin and culminating in death followed by reincarnation. In their nature religion there simply is no place for so sinister a figure as Satan. That term, incidentally, was later applied to the devil. It comes from the ancient

Hebrew concept of god's counterplayer, or rather the personification of the destructive in nature.

The accused witches were inevitably forced to confess to the weirdest activities, which, under torture, they readily enough did. Riding through the air on broomsticks, for instance, which the Church inquisitors thought witches habitually did, was actually a misinterpretation of two separate and very real customs. At the gatherings of the country folk, the women would bring their brooms as symbols of domestic virtue. They would then ride around the sacred circle astride the brooms ceremoniously, after which they would jump a few times with their brooms. The idea of this "sympathetic magic" was to "show the grain how high to grow." Whenever witches could not attend a nocturnal rite they would anoint themselves with a hallucinogenic salve made from nightshade, belladonna, and other delusion-producing herbs. Although their imaginations soared high and their fantasies were fierce, these witches actually never left their beds.

Nor do witches ever practice the Black Mass, a blasphemous mockery of the real Mass. Since witches do not accept Christianity in the first place, they would hardly mock a faith they do not believe in. Those who perform Black Masses are thrill seekers and certainly not witches.

There are fertility rites in witchcraft celebrations. Witches, as a rule, work in the nude. This is part of their belief in the sacred forces of nature, life, death, and rebirth, and is in no way lustful or evil.

Due to the persecutions, witchcraft went underground and only the so-called hereditary witches continued to practice their ancient faith in private, ever fearful of being found out.

By the dawn of the nineteenth century, the age of reason had also dawned in respect to witchcraft persecutions, and they were finally left alone. But so deeply had the Church left her mark upon these unfortunate people that freedom from persecution did not automatically encourage their return to the light. It was not until 1951, when the ancient Witchcraft Act was finally repudiated in Britain, that the Craft established itself once again aboveground. To be sure, the few hereditary witchcraft families that had survived all those centuries of persecution were not exactly eager to invite strangers to their rituals or go on television. Social discrimination remains.

In America, the best-known witch-hunt had its origin in a comparatively minor event: in the 1690's in Massachusetts, the West Indian servant girl of one of Salem's leading citizens displayed some psychic abilities, including trance mediumship. To the superstitious and untrained Puritans, this seemed the work of the devil. The girl was pressured into admitting a compact with the Prince of Darkness, and, faced with mortal danger, decided to pull a few respectable ladies of the community down with her. Before long the hysteria had spread all over Salem, and dozens of people were on trial as witches in league with Satan. The very people who had come to America to escape persecution for *their* religious beliefs sat in judgment over them! By comparison with European holocausts, the number of victims at Salem was small. Eventually, every one of the accused was exonerated by a court of inquiry, which did not bring them back to life, of course.

The shame of Salem doesn't seem to prevent enterprising press agents from using that ancient wrong to promote a current project. *Bewitched* is a highly entertaining, if totally unrealistic, television program dealing with the kind of witches that never were. Played by Elizabeth Montgomery and Agnes Moorehead, the two chief witches decided to visit Salem, Massachusetts, in July 1970 to grab a little free newspaper space.

A lot less harmless was the recent case of one Frank Daminger, Jr., who filed suit against ten former neighbors in Weirton, West Virginia, for having destroyed his reputation by calling him "a male witch, warlock, and devil's consort." Apparently, Daminger performed certain rituals, at least one of which took place in a cemetery. He made claims of possessing supernatural powers, according to witnesses, although no one reports having seen him actually work. Evidently, Mr. Daminger, a horse trainer by profession, didn't find being called a witch funny or beneficial to his trade. He put a $150,000 price tag on his reputation—or, rather, his attorneys did. However, it all ended in mutual apologies and explanations. The *Cincinnati Inquirer* covered the trial extensively in its October 29, 1971, issue and in subsequent issues. This proves, if nothing else, that the accusation of witchcraft, whether proven or not, is still a potent subject for the public prints. Even the Iron Curtain countries have their problems along those lines. According to an Associated Press dispatch of May 11, 1969, six villagers from around Szeged, Hungary, went on trial for calling an elderly woman a witch. The woman had been accused of casting an evil eye on a young man who was courting her granddaughter, and the villagers threatened to hang her.

Far more serious was the result of such an accusation near Zurich, Switzerland. In January 1969, six members of a religious sect led by a defrocked priest and a fifty-four-year-old spinster were accused of flogging a girl named Bernadette Hasler to death in May 1966. They had accused the seventeen-year-old girl of having links with "the devil Lucifer," and the girl died as the result of beatings and torture.

Despite our enlightened age and the supposed freedom of worship and thought, there are still those among us who would suppress the unorthodox, the different, that which is of the minority. A lady wrote to me from Wisconsin after she had studied my book *The Truth About Witchcraft*. She was perplexed by finding in her set of *World Books* that witchcraft was therein described as follows: "Witchcraft is the practice of evil acts by witches. A witch's power was believed to have been given or sold by devils. But witchcraft caused much suffering before civilization substituted reason for ignorance." And the lady from Wisconsin adds, "How do you explain this? Should it not be rectified? Confused. C.F."

The *New York Times*, a generally fair and respectable paper, undertook a survey of witchcraft in its October 31, 1969, issue. The choice of that date aligns the *Times* solidly with the more sensational press such as the *Daily News* and local papers throughout the United States. Interviews with Mrs. Raymond Buckland, Sybil Leek, and a local witch, Florence S. of Brooklyn, of whom I had never heard before, are featured in this piece, which is hardly a survey but merely interviews with two or three available people in the Craft. The kind of journalistic brush-off usually given to any serious explanation of what Neopaganism and witchcraft really are like can also be gleaned from a letter to the editor published in *Time* magazine on April 18, 1969. Dennis Bolling, who had been one of the subjects of an earlier article on astrology and the occult, complained that he and his work had been grossly misrepresented. The letter of rectification was one paragraph long; the original article took several pages. And a Los Angeles housewife named Louise Huebner is fighting the county authorities for the right to use the title "official witch of Los Angeles County" given to her in a weak moment by county authorities when her publicity value was being much appreciated in various public causes. Mrs Huebner is the author of two books dealing rather loosely with various aspects of witchcraft—at least the way she understands the term, which may not be quite what initiates would accept. Nevertheless, Louise Huebner makes no secret of her witchery. The papers are having fun with her, especially as she does not insist on becoming too serious.

But who then are the true heirs of Wicca? Not those who mistake a little ESP or an odd pyschic experience for genuine witchcraft, nor those self-styled witches who think casting spells is all-important, and learning the esoteric and spiritual secrets of the Old Religion too complicated to undertake. Some witches are born; others find their way into the Craft at the right time, when they have a need to belong to it. The hereditary witch may well leave her ancestral religion now and again, although this doesn't happen frequently. Those who become converts to witchcraft jealously guard their newly won prerogatives from the curious and idle thrill seekers. Motivation, background, one's attitude toward the universe, morality, society, love, the need to relate to similarly minded people—these are the elements by which one can judge whether or not a person *should* be a witch. Ever since I wrote *The Truth About Witchcraft* hundreds of people have approached me to show them the way to the nearest coven. Some of these are youngsters in their early teens, and I could not introduce them to witchcraft groups even if I wanted to. But to those over eighteen I sometimes give a hint, or even an introduction, if I think that they would make good witches and that the covens would gain useful members in them.

*

Who are the people who want to become witches and why? Diane M. is a nineteen-year-old student at a Southern university. She is a lovely blonde enjoying all the usual pastimes nineteen-year-old blondes at major universities enjoy, but to her this is not enough. For as long as she can remember, she has had a strong interest in witchcraft. To her, "magic" was the most important thing in the world, even though her parents told her there was no such thing. She tried ESP experiments but got very little out of them. Then she veered toward yoga, which met her needs somewhat more but not the need for sharing with others her beliefs in a nature religion. These beliefs included reincarnation and the conviction that there exists a power within all of us which can be used for good if we only know how to tap it.

Much of her time is spent outdoors walking, riding, painting, or writing. A member of the Episcopal Church, she soon became disillusioned with that faith because, to her, it yielded no results and left her feeling powerless. "I only want to be with others who believe as I do who can teach me more about my chosen religion," she explained.

Diane thinks that perhaps in a previous life she was a priestess and some of these memories are now the driving force in
her life. Her fiancé also shares her interests, and they both
asked me to introduce them to a coven in their area. She added
that she was willing to wait and study diligently, to keep secrecy,
that neither her fiancé nor herself had any nudity hangups and
both were quite sincere in their quest for Wicca.

Larry B. was a monk for ten years. After reading my book on
witchcraft, he contacted me feeling that "the Old Religion" had
more to offer him than the Catholic Church. Betty F. of New
Mexico explained that she was currently being initiated into
a local coven and wanted to subscribe to the British publication *The Pentagram*. R.C.H. is a clinical instructor and does
social work in New England. Of European extraction, he is in
his middle forties, is married, and has a family. He contacted
me for information leading to a coven in his area. Susan B.
and her husband invited me to dinner at their home in Los
Angeles to discuss their common interest in witchcraft. I
couldn't find the time for that, but I did introduce them to
Martha Adler, priestess of the nearest coven. "I'm what is
called a white witch. I do not indulge in satanism in any form
whatsoever and I have never used my gift for evil," explains
Peggy B. As well she might, since she is only fifteen years old.
She has already lectured on witchcraft at her school and used
her psychic abilities to demonstrate to her friends that there
are more things in heaven and earth than the majority of fif-
teen-year-olds know about. Kay, an Ohio girl, believes that there
is one being which guides us in our days, and that the being is
not like the God she has learned of in church but more a
power within. She wants to be able to help people in trouble
and at the same time free her own soul from uncertainties and
struggles. For her, witchcraft holds the answer.

Dr. Douglas M. is not a neurotic thrill seeker, one of the
idle curious, nor a superstitious person. His interest in the
Craft stems from the fact that during the past few years he

has become increasingly disenchanted with Christianity. He feels that the Christian morality and faith have let the world down and that in the name of Christianity, wars, killing, injustice, and intolerance have been committed in the Western world. Dr. M. is a dentist; active in his church and in local community life, he has also published some writing and enjoys a good name in his community. To him, witchcraft represents a peaceful religion, a personal faith in which the deity is represented by the power within all of us. Mrs. L. is a Canadian mother in her middle years who always practiced her psychic abilities to help others. To her, learning about the Old Religion seemed only to confirm what she had always believed in and sought. She contacted me in the hope that I could direct her to a coven, not so much for her own self, but in order to help her son obtain better employment through witchcraft. "I no longer feel odd," she explained. "The confirmation of my instincts is very reassuring."

Kim S. is a twenty-five-year-old industrial engineer working for a naval project in the South. His wife teaches sociology at a nearby college. Born into a conservative religious family, he soon found himself wandering from one faith to the other, never finding what he searched for. He found himself particularly repelled by the Baptist faith and what to him seemed intolerance of that church. He wanted to worship a superior force, the essence of all things, and as he read more about witchcraft, he saw the simple universal truth of all religions contained in the tenets of the Craft. His own grandfather was what in the South is called a conjur' man. To his horror, on several occasions Kim has been able to make things happen, especially when he was angry. At the time it did not occur to him that that had anything to do with spells or witchcraft. In retrospect, he realizes that he unconsciously applied some of the principles contained in the teachings of the Old Religion. For instance, many years ago, when he was still in high school, he went with a certain girl for three years. Shortly before graduation,

he lost the girl to an older fellow. When Kim saw he was
losing ground, he cursed his competitor as a jealous young
man might do, thinking nothing of it. A short time later, his
erstwhile girlfriend borrowed his ring and the ring of the other
man to have them psychometrized by a local psychic. When
she returned Kim's ring, she informed him that, according to
the psychic, the other man whom she had preferred over Kim
was apparently under a powerful curse. Kim was not impressed
by this since he had not taken his own curse very seriously.
A week later the other man was removed to a mental hospital
for no apparent reason. Kim began to wonder whether his
curse had not been the cause of it. A few years later, a man
for whom he had once worked embarrassed him needlessly
in public. Angered by this display, he secretly cursed the man.
Abruptly the man's fortunes changed. Within twenty months
he went bankrupt twice. Once again Kim wondered whether
he had not been the cause of this. He resolved never to allow
hatred and anger to well up in him again but to use such
powers as he might have only for good.

*

Gail is twenty-one and lives with her family in Arkansas.
She is an artist and likes to write. As with most people intent
on becoming witches, the quest for the Old Religion in no way
is a substitute for love, affection, or sex. Everyone who has
contacted me to learn more about witchcraft or to be introduced
to a group practicing it has turned out to be a well-balanced
individual without romantic problems or complications. Gail
has had ESP experiences all her life, but she knows the difference between psychic phenomena and witchcraft. She has a
great sensitivity toward plants and animals and likes to see
things grow and develop. What she likes about witchcraft is
that she considers it a "do-something" religion that will help
her and others as well. She is frustrated with the life she
currently leads. She wants more to show for having lived than,
as she puts it, a list of new movies she has seen or restaurants

she has been to, and most important of all, she wants and needs to belong to a group that *understands* her. The Old Religion, she asserts, fits her, and she would like to become an asset to it. The problem, of course, is to find a coven in the area in which she lives, a problem that exists for many others who have come to me, sincere and serious in their quest for a channel of pagan expression. Even villages have several churches. The pagan movement is as yet partly underground, and where it is aboveground and has its temples and sanctuaries, they are far and few between.

*

Margaret F. lives in a Cincinnati suburb. Now in her early twenties, she has worked at odd jobs in shops here and there, and despite her simple education, has an above average intelligence. After she studied witchcraft for two years, I introduced her to the leaders of the Cincinnati coven. This group practices a mixture of Anglo-Saxon-Celtic witchcraft and Kabbalah and has held its major rituals in the countryside for fear of attracting too much attention from the not always friendly citizens of Cincinnati. Bill, one of their two leaders, had originally invited me to come and see the group and had supplied me with material concerning their activities, which I have published in *The Truth About Witchcraft*. Some of the coven members, however, did not agree with the need to explain witchcraft publicly to those who might have false concepts of it, and Margaret was accused of being too friendly with me and was consequently denied the privilege of initiation into the Cincinnati coven.

Margaret, who is unusually small, thinks she has fairy ancestry, especially on her mother's side. Her background is mainly Celtic, and it is true that among the Scottish and Irish people there persists the legend of a small race preceding the Celts in Great Britain and Ireland. These might very well have been the legendary fairy people.

While waiting for an opportunity to become a witch, Margaret took a part-time job in a local bookshop so she could read all there was to be read on the subject. Eventually, she became an initiated solitary witch, that is to say, one who practices privately and alone.

*

Mrs. Lisa C. of California thinks she is a witch because she has been casting spells for ten years, spells that have been working. In fact, her spells have been working so well that she is now teaching the spelling business to others, mostly friends. Mrs. C.'s spells aren't dangerous. When her husband failed to catch any fish on their last outing, she cast a spell on the water and presto, he caught five fish in twenty minutes. People come to her for help and she sends them out with positive thoughts. That, she thinks, is witchcraft.

Less benign is the problem of Mildred B. of Virginia. She thinks she has been the victim of a spell for a long time. She says she has asked five different "occultists" for help, and they have tried to remove the spell, but in vain. Monica L. is a student at Vassar College. She wanted to find a bona fide witch, not for evil purposes, but "for the amelioration of particular problems." According to the witch I sent her to, Mary Nesnick, the problems involved a boy friend.

*

Here we have three examples of what witchcraft is *not*. Psychic experiences, amazing though they may be to the one to whom they happen, do not make that person a witch. A desire to cast spells and circumvent the laws of nature is also insufficient grounds to become involved with the Old Religion. While there is room in witchcraft for love potions and incantations of a romantic nature, they must be grounded in far deeper relationships than the desire simply to influence someone who is cool to one's advances. Just to use the gimmicks and tricks of the magic that comes from being a witch would be a disservice to the cause of the Old Religion. The outer manifestations of belonging to the Craft follow naturally once the inner meanings have been grasped.

*

I have mentioned here a few of those who have contacted me in the recent past with a desire to become witches. Now let me tell you of some who have indeed become witches after I became convinced of their sincerity and the seriousness of their purpose. I should hasten to explain that I am not in the business of being a clearinghouse for would-be witches. Those who feel that they have the necessary mental and spiritual attitudes toward the Old Religion, and whose purpose is essentially to seek a new philosophy rather than the outward thrills of a magical cult, can, of course, contact me by writing. It would be wise to include as many details as possible about oneself and one's reasons for wanting to be put in touch with a coven or an initiated witch. If the seeker is at least eighteen years of age, is single or has the consent of his or her mate in this quest, then perhaps an occasional contact can be established.

*

Patricia F. is an X-ray technician in her early thirties and lives in a small town on the West Coast. She is currently also studying at a police academy to become a deputy sheriff and has an average educational background. She is quiet, soft-spoken, and somewhat shy. She had explained to me that there was a special reason why she wanted to become a witch.

"What religion did you grow up in?"

"In the Catholic religion."

"What aspect of witchcraft do you find particularly attractive?"

"Something that goes deeper than my own religion; I think I can get more benefit out of it."

"Do you have any ESP?"

"No, I don't."

"Have you ever been to any lectures dealing with witchcraft?"

"No."

"Have you ever met anyone who was an actual witch?"

"No, I haven't."

"You wrote to me about doodling a pentagram. How did this happen?"

"Whenever I'm writing or trying to think at my desk and have a pencil in my hand, I just make that star."

"Have you ever had any memories of having lived before?"

"I *think* I was dropped from a great height, and dropped into a body of water in another life."

"Is this a recurrent impression?"

"Yes."

"In a dream state or in the waking state?"

"In both."

"Is it always the same?"

"Yes, it is."

"Do you see yourself?"

"Yes, I do. I'm in brown, a long dress, and a kind of peasant blouse."

"Does your face look different from your present face?"

"Yes, it does."

"And you feel yourself falling?"

"Yes."

"From a great height into water, you said. Then what follows?"

"Nothing."

"Are your hands bound in any way?"

"Yes, they are. Both my hands and feet."

"Are there any other recurrent impressions or dream impressions?"

"Yes."

"When did you first have this recurrent impression of falling or being thrown from a great height? At what age?"

"I must have been about twenty-five."

"Do you want to know whether you might have been someone in a previous existence connected with this?"

"Yes, I would like to know."

"You say you had a habit of *clenching your fist, with three fingers bent tightly and the thumb and little finger extended?*"

"When I'm walking in the hospital hall and I just go like this, you know, just casually—"

"Were you aware that this is a witch greeting?"

"I didn't know it until I read your book."

I then hypnotized and regressed Patricia F. gradually, past birth, where she would meet her "earlier self" in the distant past.

"Can you see the woman in the brown dress?" I finally asked.

"Yes, I do."

"I want you to go back now, before she is falling into the water. Tell me who she is and where she lives."

"I see her walking down a cobblestone road."

"Does everybody say she's a witch?"

"Yes."

"Who is the one that accuses her?"

"It's a man in black."

"After he accuses her, what is happening?"

"She runs screaming, and everyone runs after her. They catch her. They tie her up. They take her to a mill town. They have her sitting on something and—they raise it up."

"And then what do they do?"

"Let it drop."

"And then what happens to her?"

"Drowns."

"And what is the name of the town?"

"I think it's Salem."

"What is the year?"

"Fifteen forty-one."

"What country are we in?"

"England."

"I want you to go close to this woman now; I want you to look at her. Are you that woman?"

"Yes, I am."

*

Several months later, Patricia F. was initiated into the preliminary grade of a local California group practicing a pagan religion. There was a glow on her face when it was all over that I hadn't noticed before. Her shyness seemed lessened, and she spoke freely about the need to live in harmony with nature around us. Why had I helped her among the many who came to me with identical wishes? Perhaps because Patricia F. represents the average American of solid background who can do much to help others like herself understand the true tenets of paganism.

*

I met Linda about two years ago in San Francisco. We had corresponded prior to our meeting. Her letters, which came to me among hundreds of letters dealing with the subject, immediately stood out—not only because of her expressive handwriting and artistic flair, but because of her poetic approach to the inner meaning of witchcraft as she saw it. Without any formal initiation on her part, without any actual contact with witches or members of the Old Religion, she seemed to sense that she should be part of it and asked that I help her find both herself and her relation to this old cult.

"What did you think witchcraft could do for you?" I asked.

"Guide me to inner peace, and solve the problems and turmoils of the unknown in my mind. I felt that in the Craft the answers would be found."

"Did you feel that it would also resolve your professional life, and perhaps give you magic powers with which you could improve it?"

"No."

"Did you think that being a witch would cause difficulties in the community in which you live?"

"No."

"What is your background?"

"My family is upper-class, established, wealthy, materialistic."

"Did your father know about your interest in the occult?"

"No."

"Does he now?"

"Yes."

"Does he approve?"

"No."

"Do you care?"

"No."

The laconic tone of her interview with me belied the poetic tone of her written communications. Linda has read anything and everything dealing with witchcraft and the occult in general that she can put her hands on. She heads up the back-order list at the local bookstore. Her daredevil thirst for knowledge in these areas seems to have blotted out those forces within her that would normally apply themselves toward a successful career or a better home life. She is a divorcée with a small child, living in a small town, traveling very little and restricting her circle of friends to those who can instruct her in esoteric matters. Eventually, I introduced her to Sára Cunningham in Pasadena. Sára had spent many years as a teacher of Wicca, but shortly after Linda met her, Sára herself discovered the Egyptian Isis religion and devoted most of her energies to it. Consequently, Linda found that the Egyptian form of worship suited her nature and personality better, and she became one of Sára Cunningham's pupils.

What involvement with a deeply esoteric religion of this kind will do to her adjustment to the harsh realities of everyday life no one can foretell, but if Christian religious life can, on occasion, be a refuge from worldliness for those who so decide, there is no reason why a pagan cult cannot also supply this kind of need. Most people who choose Wicca do so because they want their regular, everyday lives improved upon or because they want to understand the forces of nature better. Linda joined the Egyptian temple to find an emotional outlet more suitable to her imagery and poetic detachment from reality than the cold, drab Establishment religions could possibly offer her. If it works for her, then it is all to the good.

*

The opposite view of the blessings of witchcraft is represented by Robert Carson, who works in public relations. According to columnist Earl Wilson, he is connected with a Wall Street coven that is able to influence proxy fights, prevent or influence conglomerate acquisitions, and do other things in the stock market that would make stock market expert Richard Ney's hair stand up even if there weren't any witches around. Mr. Carson sounded friendly enough. The meeting place and location of his Wall Street coven has, however, remained shrouded in obscurity.

Another Earl Wilson-featured witch is actress Cindi Bulak. Cindi is a pretty redhead in her middle twenties. She is from Chicago and has a Polish background. Her witchcraft broke into public print when the press agent for *Celebration*, the musical she was appearing in, introduced her to Earl Wilson, who may not know anything about witches but certainly knows a lot about girls. When all the chitchat had evaporated, Cindi and I discussed her witchcraft seriously. The group she belonged to at the time we met was a group of suburbanites in Port Washington, Long Island. They were "traditionals" and used their Craft merely for so-called white purposes—to improve each other's health and business chances, and in general to promote a better life for themselves. But even Cindi couldn't keep the show from closing.

Rita Norling is a somewhat commercial witch of Russian background who lives with her two young sons near Sunset

Boulevard in Hollywood. She does a thriving business in aromatic oils, incense, and perfumes, all of which she calls "curios"
so as not to get in trouble with the law, which in California
can be nasty at times, especially when it comes to the occult.
Rita's products have such tantalizing names as Easy Life Brand
Oil, Genuine Irresistible Brand Oil, Cleopatra Brand Incense,
and Repellent Brand Oil. She also markets Genuine Do-it
Love Brand Powder, which her catalogue states is not always
available, and even floor washes, such as Money Drawing Brand
Floor Wash. Quite obviously, Rita does not take her witchcraft
and commercial products too seriously. I met her over dinner
in Hollywood and found her to be a charming, well-read woman
whose humorous approach to the Old Religion apparently did
not cause her any pangs of conscience. Underneath her com-
mercialism, she is a true pagan, but she prefers to keep the
esoteric aspects of her religious beliefs to herself. She goes to
great pains to explain that the articles she sells do not impart
any miraculous powers to anyone. Which is only right. You
can't become a witch by proxy.

Also in the Los Angeles area, Martha and Fred Adler's coven
continues to be active in spurts. At the moment Martha is
taking a "postgraduate" course with Sára Cunningham. Although she had been made a priestess by mail and long-distance
instruction by the leaders of Cincinnati coven, Martha evidently
feels the need for higher teachings. She and Fred, who often
acts as her high priest, have put together what they call "the
11th through 20th commandments." Here they are:

11. Thou shalt worship no idols of thine own creation, nor
those created by the society in which thee live.

12. Honor thyself, whereby you cannot dishonor another.

13. Thou shalt not break a man's ricebowl.

14. Thou shalt not step on another's koa.

15. Thou shalt see others as in a mirror; for there, but for
the grace of the Fates, goest thee.

16. Thou shalt honor the integrity and thoughts of another; for, remote as it may seem, he may be right and thee may be wrong.

17. Thou shalt not covet; for, though the grass is greener in the other pasture, this is an illusion of the mind.

18. Thou shalt not be vengeful, for vengeance begets vengeance, to the time of infinity.

19. Thou shalt be colorblind, for all men are green.

20. Do as thou wilt, an ye harm no other. That is the whole of the LAW.

Until recently, Joseph Wilson edited a witchcraft newsletter called *The Waxing Moon*. Would-be witches could glean a great deal of useful information from this simple newsletter, published in Topeka, Kansas. I understand, however, that the Wilsons have since removed to England.

In New York City the oft-mentioned Mary Nesnick is currently leading a small coven of Gardnerian witches. They worship on all the traditional holidays and, whenever the temperature allows, in the open. They are traditionally skyclad, too, which means naked. "Let us not be discordant in the faith," Mary said to me at our last meeting when we discussed the frequent bickering among witches as to who had the true approach to the Old Religion. It is difficult to determine who is the author of some of the spells and incantations that Mary Nesnick uses in her services. Some are certainly old. Others may have been written or rewritten by the priestess herself.

Diana

Twilight is over, and the moon in might
Draws to its zenith, as beyond the stream
Dance the wild witches, fair as a dream
In a garden, naked in Diana's sight.

Flaming censer on the sweet altar, bright
Gleaming on the water, drifting vapours teem,
Laughter and swaying white shoulders gleam
Oh joy and wonder at their lovely sight!

Prayer to the Goddess

Thou art the Great Mother who giveth birth
Who shall escape from thy power?
Thy form is an eternal mystery
Thou makest it plain in the Summerland
And on the earth.
Command the sea and the sea obeyeth
Through thee a tempest becometh a calm
Command the waters of the earth
And thy will shall arrest the floods
I shall say hail O Great Queen and Mother!

Who would have thought that there was a growing coven up
Alaska way, what with the kind of clothes true witches do not
wear? The climate doesn't seem to lend itself to it, at least not
outdoors. But that doesn't seem to have stopped a small but
enthusiastic group of Wicca followers from studying witchcraft
and practicing it. It was all started not long ago by Kristine F.
in Anchorage. The group's main purpose was to work various
healing spells. One of the "operations" they attempted recently was to make a blind woman see and to help someone to
live who had been given up by medical doctors. As it happened,
they were successful in both instances. With her husband Rick
and another couple, Jerry and Mia, plus a young man who
happened to be in the area, they worshiped in the old Dianic
way. Jerry, an artist, made the altar himself, while his wife
Mia did some of the painting of the magical symbols for it.

Kristine first became interested in witchcraft while in high
school. She read whatever was available in the local library
but soon realized that most of it was fiction—and bad fiction

at that. When she joined a local metaphysics group, she met another lady who shared her interest in the Old Religion. Three months later they started Alaska's first coven of Diana. Their meetings are every Saturday at midnight. Since Kristine is also psychic, inevitably some ESP entered the services, and on one occasion, she assures me, the spirit of Aleister Crowley himself manifested itself and created a great deal of disturbance in her house. For a while she became almost obsessed with the late author, who has often been called "the bad boy of witchcraft" because of his outrageous views on society, sex, and mores. Eventually, Kristine explains, she got rid of the possessive spirit of Mr. Crowley, thanks to the Mother Goddess, Diana.

*

Dennis is a nineteen-year-old soldier from Michigan who is stationed in Alaska and boards with Rick and Kristine. Last Candlemas he joined the coven officially. Jerry and Mia have six children, ranging in age from six to seventeen, who have been brought up in the ways of Wicca and in metaphysics in general. Jerry works in a warehouse of a large moving and storage company, and his wife teaches free classes in healing whenever she has the chance. In their Saturday night rituals, they use Alex Sanders' initiation service as a basic source, but they have added prayers of their own to it. After consecrating the circle, group meditation, and prayers, the members of the coven join hands and sing the witches' rune. This in turn is followed by their healing circle, then the consecration of the Sabbath cakes and wine, which they all share inside the circle. Originally from California, Jerry and Mia find Alaska, with its strong accent on raw nature, particularly suitable to witchcraft, or vice versa.

*

In Chicago, there is a Gardnerian coven headed by Donna Cole and Herman Enderle. Donna has been to England and

is friendly with most of the London covens. Herman, who is
of Anglo-Saxon background, stresses the Celtic-English aspects
of the Craft in his rituals and teachings. Donna explained
to me that the rituals aren't as fancy or as perfect as some
of those that I might have witnessed, but they get excellent
results in their healing services and other magical work just
the same. Their coven numbers about seven people, who meet
at each other's homes at the usual times—the four Great Sabbaths and eight lesser holidays, but always on Saturdays. Once
in a while, they drive out into the countryside for an outdoor
ritual if the weather permits, which in the Chicago area is
certainly not the case for a large portion of the year. They
wear black robes with nothing underneath for their rituals, although Donna freely admits she has also worked nude. They
are at great pains to get the witchcraft image away from
satanism, with which it is sometimes identified in the public's
mind.

On a Friday in February I met the entire group in Herman
Enderle's apartment. Except for Donna, who wore a hooded,
symbol-covered robe, everyone was casually attired. This was,
of course, a discussion evening and not a ritual.

Here are the views of Donna Cole and Herman Enderle of
Chicago, and my readers will realize that they do not differ
greatly from views held by other pagan groups:

"A pagan refuses to believe that mankind is born innately
sinful, and realizes that the concept of 'sin' is harmful to human
nature.

"We realize the powers of the universe, sometimes called
'gods,' exist not apart from but as a part of man.

"These powers may be contacted, directed, and benefit gained
from them, if man first learns to live in harmony with himself
and the universe.

"The movements of these natural forces, called 'tides' by
many, directly affect our lives, the evolution of humanity, and
the course of direction of the manifested universe.

"The pagan celebrates this force movement, in fact unifies with it, through the calendar of the year which we call the greater and lesser festivals.

"These festivals are attuned to the tides, and also reflect the eternal problems of man as he has moved forward upon the path of light.

"The pagan recognizes, and harmonizes with, the law of nature called polarity.

"We know that that which is above is that which is also below.

"There is no heaven except that which we ourselves make, and likewise there is no hell.

"Harmony with, and direction of, the great natural forces is called *magic*.

"Paganism is not fixed or dogmatic.

"We know of the existence of the spark of life that is within us that does not die, and that returns again and again until it has evolved to that which we call the eternal existence above all existences.

"We abide by the great rule of love, and that one may do as he wishes as long as it harms no other."

*

The heirs of Wicca certainly include one Leo Louis Martello, a bearded young militant witch who publishes the WICA *Newsletter*, which stands for Witches International Craft Associates. (Lest I be inundated with requests for this publication, one can obtain it from Hero Press at 153 West 80th Street in New York City.) Martello, who has the title of doctor and whose assistant is a comely young lady from New Jersey by the name of "Witch Hazel," also lectures widely on witchcraft, dressed in a black cape and using various paraphernalia, and all in all making it a very colorful occasion. Hazel assists him by simply appearing and looking pretty, which she does well indeed. Both of them are at great pains to explain that they are "continental witches." Martello himself is of Sicilian background and explains that his ancestors on his mother's side were all "strega" type people, that is to say, Italian witches.

On Hallowe'en night 1970 he called for a "witch-in" in New York's Central Park. Lest authorities take a dim view of such a gathering, he made it plain that this was not a bona fide Sabbath, but merely "a free-style esbat," or social gathering of witches. He urged all those wishing to appear to wear costumes, capes, bring candles and incense and food, and have a good time in general. He admonished those who were already coven members to leave their athames, ritual swords, and definitely their cauldrons at home. The City of New York, nevertheless, took a dim view and refused him a permit. A witch-in, the Parks Department explained, would not serve the purposes of the park. Martello, not about to be put off, explained that in that case his people would congregate as individuals, whereupon the Parks Department spokesman threatened that he would inform the police. Modern witches, especially the continental kind, do not take kindly to being threatened, but instead of convoking a grand coven to exorcise the threatened intervention, Leo Martello called the American Civil Liberties Union and with their help managed to get permission to hold his witch-in after all.

Leo Martello publishes the actual names and addresses of many of those interested in the Craft, which is remarkable for any witchcraft publication. He doesn't state whether they are initiates or merely interested in becoming members of a coven, but presumably he has their permission to do so. He calls this the "witches' encounter bureau" and listings go for one dollar apiece. There is even a questionnaire, which future members of witchcraft are supposed to fill in. The questions are intelligent and do show that Martello is genuinely interested in helping only those who have the proper motives and wishes to discourage curiosity seekers or worse. He also makes it plain that work and time has to be put in before anyone can become a member of the Old Religion. Certainly this is no racket of the kind some of the minor Christian denominations operate, where for fifty dollars or even less you can become a minister overnight. As for his able assistant, who calls herself "Witch Hazel," some time back I had the pleasure of taking her with me to a Boston television show dealing with witchcraft. She turned out to be a somewhat frightened young girl, working toward becoming an actress but actually earning her living as a waitress. To her, expressing herself in the bizarre way of continental witchcraft seemed to be not only a religious and cult experience but an outlet for submerged and suppressed emotional talents. In a way, it was a kind of acting out of something far removed from her ordinary, daytime self. Hazel has had a fair amount of ESP experiences over the years and does the publicity bit rather well, enjoying every moment of it as any pretty young girl naturally would. How much she knows of the deeper meanings of ritual I was unable to determine, for Hazel is essentially shy and introverted despite the trappings of cape, black leotards, miniskirt, and the oversize pentagram around her neck.

Martello has some more down-to-earth views on what witchcraft is all about. The motive makes the Craft either good or bad. Any true witch wouldn't permit any evil done to him without fighting back. Self-defense is a moral right. No turning the other cheek, but then, how many Christians do? There is even a witches' liberation movement, part of his Witches International Craft Associates and patterned along the lines of the other women's liberation movements. In between little blurbs for some of his many booklets on various occult subjects, Dr. Martello also notices and reviews other books he finds useful for those reading his newsletter. Martello himself is a practicing psychic, an expert in handwriting analysis and a pretty keen journalist. He has been a member of a local coven since 1953. One of the less publicized but, I think, rather important tasks the formidable Martello has set for himself is to force various encyclopedias and dictionaries to rewrite their definitions of witchcraft, eliminating the falsehoods, the linking of witchcraft with the devil and Black Masses. While I doubt that the Establishment dictionaries are going to pay much attention to such pressures, I do agree with Martello that there is hardly any printed source, other than books written by those who genuinely know witchcraft practices, that describes the Old Religion truthfully, and this helps perpetuate prejudices and falsehoods held over from the medieval times of persecution.

The Jews of this century fought many of the fabrications of an anti-Semitic nature, such as the infamous "Protocols of the Elders of Zion," purporting to herald Jewish intent to take over the world. A dedicated witch could take on the falsehoods published in secular publications dealing with witchcraft.

*

The heirs of Wicca are not only more numerous in Great Britain, but their traditions are older, more sure of themselves, and their varieties of ritual also greater. It is a proper religion for Britain, going well with the mystic climate and the general toned-down emotional reaction toward the deity. That does not mean that British witches do not work up emotional steam in their rites—quite to the contrary—but on the outside, at least, they are very English, even if they are witches. American witches tend to become militant or unduly secretive, going to extremes in their espousal or defense of the Old Religion, while their British cousins take these matters more naturally and do not fight as hard to make their point of view known. By the same token, outsiders do not sneer at followers of witchcraft in England the way Americans often do. The British have always known that witches walk among them, and while they may shake their heads in puzzlement that anyone would want to be, and be called, a witch, or, if they are righteous followers of the Church of England, perhaps mumble darkly, "The vicar ought to do something about these people," they do not get unduly steamed up over them, and the age of witchcraft persecutions is definitely over in Britain.

Foremost among the more colorful practitioners of the Old Religion in England is high priest Alexander Sanders, whose rituals I have attended many times. Recently, Sanders has somewhat replaced Sybil Leek in the public eye, probably because of his television appearances and, in no small measure, of two books, my recent *The Truth About Witchcraft* and another book about him written several years ago but only recently published called *The King of the Witches*, by June Johns. As with any controversial figure entering the limelight, Sanders has enemies and admirers. Among the more conservative followers of witchcraft he is anathema because he speaks freely publicly about his beliefs and practices. He has even been accused by some of exacting large sums of money from those desirous of becoming witches. I know of very little money changing hands in his classes, where he teaches the elements of Wicca to small groups of students, who come once a week and eventually become postulants for one of his covens. If Sanders were really swimming in money, I doubt that he would continue to serve as a superintendant of a modest building in London's Notting Hill Gate section, living in a basement flat. By now he would have his own mansion complete with temple, at least two reception secretaries to take care of mundane matters, and be driven around in a Rolls-Royce. That is at least how some Christian prophets and "bishops" of peculiar sects operate.

One of Alexander's people is a jeweler named George Alexander. He supplies witches and those joining a coven with the appropriate jewelry, most of it handmade of silver. A look at his privately circulated price list shows little indication of great profits in keeping with the Craft tradition that one may not enrich oneself unduly from its practices.

*

Anne Slowgrove, an old friend of mine who is what I called a "Druidic witch," though she herself does not use this term, has not always agreed with my interpretation of what I hear and see in witchcraft. "Tolerance and cooperation between all pagans is most important," she said to me firmly, "especially as we have had different and individual experiences in the Craft. Even members of the Craft do not agree on their terms. We need some more words to separate the different traditions which do not insult the various factions. People are bound to value their own practice above that of others."

Anne finds herself in close agreement with the editor of *Quest*, a mimeographed magazine-type newsletter published by Marian Green under the unfortunate business name Spook Enterprises at 38 Woodfield Avenue, London W. 5. *Quest* is a quarterly. Among the interesting articles in this magazine is one on "Consecration for Beginners" and one on the "Survival of the British Mysteries" by Anne Slowgrove. In addition to *Quest*, the same editor has also published two handbooks, or rather booklets, called *A Hundred Questions on Ritual Magic Answered by a Practioner of the Art* and *A Hundred Questions on Witchcraft Answered by a Member of the Craft*. Since these booklets represent but one faction in the Old Religion, the information therein is not necessarily correct for one and all. But I found them valuable sources of present-day thinking on the subject of witchcraft as it is practiced in Great Britian.

*

The words "witch" and "witchcraft" seem to bother a few people who would like to practice the essence of the Old Religion without being called witches and thus escape the social stigma of being one of those persecuted for so many centuries. Since these people could not think of a more appropriate name for their newly founded cult, they chose the name "Regency," implying that they were merely holding the place until the rightful leader came along and gave the cult its proper name. The Regency is the brainchild of an art teacher named Ronald "Chalky" White. Together with a friend, George Winter, a clerical worker, he was celebrating Hallowe'en at a local pub when they decided to start a new religion. This was in 1966, and at the present time there are over one hundred members. The Regency has neither dogma, creed, nor real leaders. To them the gods are only an extension of one's own psyche. If one suppresses part of that self, one offends the gods. Likewise, if you offend the gods, you really hurt yourself. Their main deity is the Mother Goddess, just as in witchcraft. Their meetings are held at what they call the "old times," the times of the equinoxes, at Candlemas, May Eve, Midsummer, Lammas, Hallowe'en, Midwinter, and Twelfth Night.

"We never went in for the witchcraft idea of taking our clothes off," Chalky White explained when we met near his school in Hampstead, "but we do go in for rituals, prayers, dancing around the Maypole, and we do have thirteen main members at the big meetings." To me, it appears that Regency is merely another form of Gardnerian witchcraft for those who want to eat their occult cake and have it too, socially speaking.

*

"What's in a name?" When that name is witchcraft, a great deal. Gloria Ortega, an American of Mexican ancestry, lives at Hermosa Beach, California. She and her family had to move from her former headquarters because it went up in flames of mysterious origin. I drove down with a friend from Los Angeles recently to visit her in a two-story wooden house not far from the beach—a house filled with seashells, books, candles, statues of such diverse figures as Baphomet, the goat-headed god of the witches, and St. Jude. Gloria Ortega's living room gives the impression of a tent from the *Arabian Nights*. Thick carpets cover the floors; a brazier stands in front of a main altar, ostensibly Christian. But mixed in with these seemingly normal objects—normal in any Mexican-American home—there are little telltale objects showing quite clearly that Miss Ortega belongs among the pagans. Quite clearly, too, she was careful at first because she did not know me very well. By the time we parted company later that afternoon, we were fast friends. I had heard of her originally through Martha Adler, priestess of a coven in Los Angeles.

"You used to have a shop called The Spell," I began the conversation. "I hear it burned down. Was it an accident?"

"No, it was burned down purposely. I had received several threatening notes accusing me of being a witch. Finally this fellow burned down the house."

"You *know* who did it?"

"Yes. He's in jail right now."

"What was destroyed at the time?"

"Everything. It was a total loss."

"What did you have in the shop?"

"I had at least two hundred different kind of herbs and oils, and things that I had collected for years and years, and keepsakes from my aunt. My aunt was a fortune-teller. I had books that are very hard to get, and books that she had written, also, in her own handwriting. Everything was lost in the fire. And the paintings, done of me by various artists. All of it went."

"You are a native of Los Angeles?"

"Yes. I went to school here, too. And then I spent three years in a convent also."

"Why did you leave it?"

"Because I found that it really wasn't where I wanted to be, you know, spiritually. I'm more involved in the Far East teachings."

"What do you do professionally? Do you teach?"

"No, I just help people and try to get them on the *right path*."

"Do you work with the tarots?"

"Yes, I do."

"What about rituals, rites, and spells, when necessary?"

"Small ones only because I believe that they can become like crutches."

"Do you do any so-called love spells to help people?"

"Yes, I do."

"I understand you will work one of those for us. What exactly will you do?"

"Well, a friend of mine named Maureen has had problems with a certain person named Jack. He left her pregnant, and she wants to draw him back to her. I will need certain things of his to make it work."

"How are you going to get Jack back to Maureen?"

"First, I set up my altar. I will use different ingredients to put *her* mind in the right state. Some people need these ingredients."

"What are they?"

"Holy thistle herb, and orrisroot, which is used for love. I put all these ingredients in an egg while I am praying. All I am doing is helping put her in the right frame of mind to work this thing for herself."

"Why the egg?"

"Since I was a little girl it was something I was taught. I believe it's like the beginning or rebirth."

"You use a fresh egg?"

"Yes, and blow the insides out; and then I put in these herbs."

"Do you put in anything belonging to the man?"

"Oh yes. Sperm, and perspiration from under the shirt—you just cut a piece out; and his picture, and some hair—anything you can get your hands on. Some girls say, how do I get his hair? Well, on the bed—there's always hair on the bed, you know."

"What about anything from the girl?"

"A drop of blood from her left hand, from her little finger."

"Anything else?"

"All the different herbs, and then we seal it up."

"This prayer, is it any particular prayer?"

"I usually have them recite, 'As this egg contains so shall your love flow unto me.' All she has to do is call his name. Belief in your own power is what makes it work. You have to be in a certain state of mind. That's why the ingredients are all used for the person, to set it up. When they're burning incense and doing this ritual every day, and concentrating, I say just do it for five minutes a day, and he will come back to you. But remember, it's not anything that I do; it's your own mind calling him to you. And the strangest things happen, like the candle will flare up, or the candle will tip over, or it will bounce up in the air."

"What are some of the ritual prayers that you use in connection with this?"

"We use a lot of prayers out of the book of Psalms, and I also use the rituals of the Marie Labeau book. She was a Negro spiritualist. It depends on how I think the person is going to react to this. Some people you have to show the book, other people you just tell them to say a certain thing. There isn't anything that's impossible."

"Can you give me the wording of the incantation you're using in the case of Maureen versus Jack?"

"The one that I am using for her is from the magic candle-burning book."

"How does it go?"

"I have her put a root in a pot and grow a plant. It can be any kind of plant, and every day as she takes care of this plant, she recites, 'As this flower grows, so shall your love be turned unto me.' And at the bottom of the pot she writes his name on parchment paper with the same little poem. I have friends who have pots all over the house with different names in them. Also, you take blood from your left hand, your little finger, and rub it on the man's hair at night; he'll never think of anybody else but you. I do different *little things* like that."

"What do you do if the man and the girl are not together?"

"It doesn't matter, because *he will come.*"

"What do you do when the girl and the man haven't slept together?"

"Then you use a picture, or you use the mind. You can

also work with the mind. The ingredients are all props. She can use the magical candle-burning, too."

"What is the magical candle made of?"

"It's a candle that is dipped in different oils, according to the purpose."

"Do you know the candles made in the shape of a man or a woman?"

"Yes, I used to have those in my shop. If the person *believes* they work, they work."

"What are some of the other rites that you might be able to perform for someone needing them, outside of the love rite?"

"There are different rituals to seek money, or to help business, if it is in bad shape. I never forget to have them say a little prayer to St. Jude. I have to sneak all those things in. I'm not going to tell anybody I'm a witch, and I'm doing this for you and I have all power. All I can do is just show them the way to make their own mind work correctly. And if their business is poor, if they are in despair and they are on the verge of a nervous breakdown, I will give them guta cola, which is an herb, to take every day. It rejuvenates your body. They have to do it as a ritual so they won't forget to do it. Then I also have them say a prayer to St. Jude, with their incense burning, and their candles, and sometimes I make them move their candles in certain directions, every day an inch one way or another, so that they're doing this ritual and they're praying to St. Jude. Actually St. Jude is the one that's helping them."

"I notice you have a figure of Baphomet out there. How does that fit in with the rites?"

"I just have it because somebody made it."

"I notice you have a cross; are you basically Catholic?"

"I'm not anything. I was baptized a Catholic, but I just believe that all paths lead to God."

"You are familar with the waxen-image technique of ritual. Do you do that?"

"I have."

"Does it work?"

"Again, yes, it does work if you believe it. I have one in my bedroom right now."

"What happens if somebody comes to you and asks you to perform a negative ritual, to hurt someone?"

"I won't do it, because then I will have to suffer all the bad karma for it."

*

Is it possible to recall an earlier existence in great detail in this life in a manner that can be checked out objectively? In a recent book called *Born Again: The Truth About Reincarnation*, I have demonstrated that it is. There seems to be some indication that people who relate to each other in one lifetime may meet again in another one, although not necessarily in the same relationships. Quite possibly this has to do with the working off of old karmic debts. Of concern here is the possibility that someone might be an ordinary person today yet may have lived as a witch in an earlier lifetime. If that could be proven, it would, of course, not only help to establish the case for reincarnation on firmer ground, but it might also conceivably throw light on witchcraft as it was practiced in earlier times.

*

With that in mind, I took somewhat more seriously than I might have otherwise a letter from a lady who lives in an average community in the Middle West, Omaha, Nebraska. Mrs. May S. had shown evidence of paranormal abilities over the years, and I have used some of her predictions in one of my previous books. But not until December 29, 1970, was I aware of her having any connection with witchcraft.

Mrs. S. is a grandmother, though she is only in her middle years. Her husband is a baker, and they have seven children. She is not particularly extroverted or outstanding in any way, and her appearance, speech, education, and general knowledge

belie any connection with the occult. She has certainly never
sought it consciously.

On that day in December she apparently became conscious of
a dream dealing with witchcraft. She thought it had to do
with Scotland and that those who were gathered with her in
some sort of ritual wore long capes and hoods that covered
their faces. For some reason, she connected me in an earlier
lifetime with this dream. Since Mrs. S. had read many of
my books and apparently was a genuine fan of mine, I did not
pay too much attention to this asserted connection. But if she
had indeed had recollections of an earlier lifetime as a witch, she
should have intimate knowledge of rituals and details incon-
sistent with her current situation. Consequently, I invited her
to meet me in Chicago, the nearest point to her home town
I would be at in the foreseeable future. In the company of her
daughter Jennifer, she met me at the Oxford Motor Hotel in
the Loop area, where I had a suite. After a few moments of
small talk, we settled down to the business of finding out
what undiscovered layers were underneath her present self
and what connections, if any, her present person had with the
witches of old. The date was February 13, 1971, and the
time four o'clock in the afternoon. Outside the traffic in the
Loop seemed somewhat muffled as we began to delve into
Mrs. S.'s past:

"When was the first time you had any inkling of having lived
before?"

"Five years ago, when I was ironing, all of a sudden I saw
this nineteen-year-old girl; she had a strange little cap and
dress on. It didn't seem to fit our times."

"*Where* did you see this girl?"

"It seemed like a big picture in front of me; I was ironing
and yet I wasn't there. I was fully conscious. I knew that was
me, and I knew she was nineteen."

"Did you hear any voice telling you this?"

"No, I just knew it was near Boston, Massachusetts, and

that there were five people that were hanged on that day for being witches."

"Do you remember any family name or first name?"

"No, I didn't get any names. I knew that I was only nineteen, and I knew children loved me, and I knew everybody thought I was a witch because I did things that were strange, things that people couldn't explain."

"Did this girl look like you physically?"

"Somewhat, yes. She had brown hair, light blue eyes, and was pretty much my size. I knew it was *me* I was seeing."

"At the time when this occurred had you done any reading on witchcraft?"

"No, I hadn't; I didn't know anything about reincaration or witchcraft."

"Were there any other moments when you had visions of having lived before, particularly in relation to witchcraft?"

"Yes, there were. Once I saw a big iron pot over a fireplace, and I could see myself, and I'd go and look at a person who was sick. I would stand and I could see into the body, and I knew what was wrong and what to do. Then I would see myself go and get bark, or leaves, and boil them and give it to this person."

"Did you look like you look now?"

"I had brown hair and blue eyes. But I was taller and thinner. I looked different."

"How were you dressed?"

"I had a long dress on; it was kind of dingy dress."

"Did you ever see yourself taking part in any rituals?"

"Once in a dream; that was two or three months ago. There I saw myself with others, and we had these hoods on. It was all one piece, but it came around our heads and seemed to kind of tie with a drawstring and go clear down to our feet; it was of a grayish color with white in it, like a charcoal gray. All we could see were the faces. We were outside."

"What did you do?"

"Some kind of ceremony was going on, for some special occasion."

"Did you ever see yourself die because of witchcraft, or being hurt because of your beliefs?"

"No. I had lots of enemies and people were trying to harm me, but they never did. But I didn't live very long. I wasn't very old when I died."

"The vision you saw of yourself as the nineteen-year-old, and the vision where you saw yourself as a witch, do you think that was the same person? The same time and incarnation?"

"No; they seemed to be entirely different. The nineteen-year-old came much later."

*

At this point, the subject was hypnotically regressed to an earlier existence. There seemed to be no difficulty in going under, or in reaching the deeper levels of hypnotic consciousness. I regressed Mrs. S. until she came face to face with another person; this happened almost immediately.

"I see myself. I'm a girl of fourteen."

"What is your name?"

"Mary. I'm in Belfast, Ireland."

"What year are we in?"

"Seventeen thirty-two."

"I want you to come back a few years until you're a grown girl, and you have become involved with witchcraft. Tell me, can you see yourself as a grown person, and describe yourself?"

"Yes, I see myself; I'm older; I've got dark brown hair; I have greenish eyes; I'm rather a strange person."

"In which way are you strange?"

"I seem to have healing powers that are not the usual way."

"What do people call you?"

"I'm married now."

"Who are you married to?"

"Tim Olsen."

"What work does he do?"

"He's a tenor."

"Where does he sing?"

"Oxford College."

"What religion does he belong to?"

"There's something that's called Talesmen."

"What does that mean?"

"A group that is hidden; nobody knows about it but the ones that belong."

"How many are there in the group?"

"There are thirteen."

"Who's the head of it?"

"A man. I don't like him too well."

"What is his name?"

"He's my husband's brother. His name is Nils Olsen."

"Is your husband a member of this group?"

"I don't see him there."

"How many are men, and how many are women?"

"There's five men and eight women."

"Who are the other women?"

"Well, there's a Maria Olsen, too, there. I don't like her too well either. And there's a Hilda Bernstead, or Broomstead, something like that."

"Where are they all from?"

"They're from two or three places, scattered, little communities of houses."

"How often do you meet?"

"Once a month."

"On what day of the month?"

"Always when the moon is full."

"What do you do when you meet?"

"We pay homage to the Supreme Deity, and ask that we be cleansed and purified of all misdeeds and thoughts."

"How do you evoke that Supreme Deity?"

"They get into a circle and do some kind of weird dance. And they sing."

"What do they sing?"

"They're singing a song in another language."

"What language is it?"

"I don't know."

"Do you remember any of the words?"

"It's just about love, and the beauty of nature, the freeness of the soul, happiness; but love triumphs over all."

"After the song and the dance, what happens?"

"Well, by having this beautiful music and the dancing, it seems like something is stirred up, the power is far greater. Then we ask that we be cleansed and purified so we can do the work of this Supreme Being."

"How do you call the Supreme Being?"

"Mother Goddess. That's all."

"What is the next step?"

"Those who have done something real bad must go before the high priest, and he does something to free them, but I don't know what, because we look down at the ground and we don't raise our eyes."

"How are you dressed?"

"In a long cape."

"Do you wear anything else?"

"No; that's all."

"Do you have any jewelry upon you?"

"I have something around my neck. Some kind of a silver cross. A heavy one, with a certain symbol on it. We all have them. They're on leather, not a chain."

"Who is in the center of the circle?"

"It's where the high priest stands."

"How is he dressed?"

"His cape is deep purple and silver, and he has some kind of a silver thing on his head."

"What happens to the people who have come before the high priest to be cleansed of their sins?"

"He does something to their body, but I don't know what."

"Is there a priestess?"

"Yes, there is."

"Where is she standing?"

"At the opposite end of the circle."

"How is she dressed?"

"She has a green robe, and a silver thing on her head, too."

"After everyone has been before the high priest, what is the next step?"

"Then there just seems to be much rejoicing."

"How are they rejoicing?"

"They're drinking something."

"What are they drinking?"

"I think it's red wine."

"Then what?"

"Everybody's very happy. We're all free, without any sin, without anything weighing upon us. Some fall upon the ground and sleep there. In the early morning hours I go home."

"Is there anything else you do as a member of this group other than meeting once a month in the outdoors?"

"I heal people all the time."

"Do you ever use any ointment on yourself to create states of being out of the body?"

"I seem to drink things that are brewed, that taste terrible. They have real strong effects. They make me see things, and know things."

"What about the church in the village? Do they know about this group?"

"We keep it all hidden."

"Does anyone know about this group?"

"Some suspect, but they don't really know. And they can't prove anything. They try, but they can't."

"Now I want you to look for the girl with the strange cap. Can you see her?"

"Yes, I can see her."

"Who is she?"

"The name I get is Marybeth—Rawlings."

"Where does she live, and what is the year we are in?"

"She's in New Boston, Massachusetts, in the United States of America. I can't get a year."

"Ask her who's the president of the United States."

"Seems to me like she says Woodrow Wilson."

"What street does she live on?"

"Oxford Street."

"And what number?"

"Nineteen-twelve."

"What does her father do for a living?"

"I don't see either mother or father. She lives upstairs, above a shop of some kind. She seems to be all alone."

"What sort of work does she do?"

"She was a child's governess, but they caught her doing something. This little boy was very sick, and he was going to die, and she knew it, and they were gone, and she knew that she could heal him, and she did, and he lived, but they said she used witchcraft. She was seventeen then."

"Is she a witch?"

"No, she's not a witch. She has these powers. She's very unhappy and confused because these things she does are natural things, and she doesn't know what she's accused of; she doesn't understand."

"How does her life proceed from then on? How does she die?"

"She lives two more years, and it's August, and she is hanged."

"She is hanged? By whom?"

"Oh, there's two men; they put a black thing over her head, and something goes out from under her. But she doesn't care. She doesn't care at all. You know, they said—oh, this one man he's so terrible, he says if you will renounce this devil that makes you do these things, that maybe there's a chance, you know, that they might let her live. But she knows they'll kill her anyhow, and besides, it isn't a devil but God."

*

After she had returned to full consciousness, I instructed May S. to remember more and more her previous lifetimes. This is contrary to my usual procedure in which I suggest that the conversation between the hypnotized subject and me be forgotten. I wanted Mrs. S. to become conscious of previous incarnations in the hope that after we parted company, some additional material might come through either in dream form or as flash waking visions. It is a little like the loosening of the soil in gardening. Eventually, something will come up. After I brought Mrs. S. back to full consciousness, she remembered only that I had put her under. She felt rested and was quite her usual self. A little while later, she and her daughter departed to return to Omaha the following morning. On February 17, four days after our regression experiment in Chicago, May S. put down in great detail what had been dredged up from her unconscious. She now remembered clearly that she had been active in witchcraft under the name of Mary Gefuston, that her mother's name had been Alice and her father's George, and that they had lived in Sheffield in the township of Kent. The man she married, as already indicated under hypnosis, was named Tim Olsen, and his older brother was the high priest. The gatherings, always at the time of the full moon, were in a wooded area beyond a clearing. The scene was much clearer to her now than during the regression, as if I had managed to break open her storehouse of pre-natal memories.

When the group met, Mrs. S. explained, they had their capes on but took them off and were naked when the ceremony got under way. Some kind of oil was put on them, then they were in a circle singing and dancing until they reached a state of ecstasy, after which the purification and cleansing took place for those who had done some wrong deed. She also saw herself drink out of a black iron pot, a drink that gave her great psychic powers and seemed to react upon the members' sexual drive. There followed lovemaking, but everyone had to leave before dawn.

Sheffield and Kent are nowhere near each other on the English map, although there may be, of course, some obscure location by that name in Kent. Nor do the inconsistencies of Scandinavian names in Belfast and the shifting of location from Northern Ireland to England worry me too much. What is of concern here is the accurate description of witchcraft rituals. Mrs. S. has not read my book on witchcraft nor any other work dealing with the subject. I see no reason to doubt her word, as she has nothing to gain from lying to me. If indeed she has no knowledge of witchcraft rites from published sources and has not researched the subject, then her knowledge of details is remarkable for an Omaha housewife. From whatever source her information stems, it does seem to be accurate.

*

The heirs of Wicca treat their matrimony in various ways according to their own abilities and to the state of consciousness in which they as individuals find themselves. Some of those seeking to express the link with the deity within themselves through a genuine nature religion are as yet unable to shake loose some of their restrictions of modern society and the inbred puritanism which prevents some of us from expressing ourselves completely freely. There is obviously room in Wicca for many schools and many forms of worship.

In this connection, it is interesting to note that one of the more controversial features of the revived Wicca religion, worship in the nude, seems to cause problems not only to unconcerned outsiders who see in nudity license and lust, but even to those who know better. If a woolen garment is worn, then some of the bodily energy is indeed neutralized. That is not a matter of opinion but a scientific fact. Body electricity increased during the ritual will be permitted to escape at a given moment in unison with the energies of others in the group. Unquestionably, other reasons for the shedding of clothes were present in past centuries. Strangely, these reasons seem to parallel those given by some of our young people today who take their clothes off in protest against the Establishment. The closing scene of Act I in the popular musical *Hair*, the goings on at the Woodstock festival, some of the spontaneous expressions of freedom by onlookers at a recent Off Broadway production of a Julian Beck play, seemed to me similar expressions of rebellion against the falsehoods and hypocrisies of contemporary society. In general, I suspect the question of worshiping robed or nude hinges on convenience and the desire not to embarrass either timid members or neighbors.

That England's "Druidic" witches like to dress up in black robes is not surprising since they are essentially an intellectual branch of the Old Religion. I am somewhat more surprised that "continental witch" Leo Martello also prefers man-made costumes to "skyclad" worshiping. In *Aradia, the Gospel of the Witches* by Charles G. Leland, a collection of traditional writings of Dianic witchcraft in Italy that was first published in the late nineteenth century and republished by Raymond Buckland in 1968, we find some of the Italian incantations translated into ordinary English. Here, from Aradia, is the conjuration of Diana:

I do not bake the bread, nor with it salt, nor do I cook the honey with the wine; I bake the body and the blood and soul, the soul of great Diana that she shall know neither rest nor peace, and ever be in cruel suffering till she will grant what I request, what I do most desire. I beg it of her from my very heart and if the grace be granted, O Diana! in honor of thee I will hold this feast. Feast and drain the goblet deep. We will dance and wildly leap and if thou grantest the grace which I require, then when the dance is wildest, all the lamps shall be extinguished and we'll freely love! And thus shall it be done, all shall sit down to the supper, all naked, men and women, and the feast over, they shall dance, sing, make music and then love in the darkness, with all the lights extinguished; for it is the Spirit of Diana who extinguishes them, and so they will dance and make music in her praise.

To which the author, Charles Leland, remarks in the appendix, "The extinguishing of lights, nakedness, and the orgy were regarded as symbolical of the body being laid in the ground, the grain being planted, or of entering into darkness and death, to be revived in new forms, or regeneration and light. It was the laying aside of daily life."

*

In *The Green Egg*, a pagan newsletter published in St. Louis, Missouri, a rather charming, simple prayer for those who work witchcraft alone is given. It is essentially similar to the blessings one finds in most Wicca rituals, except that it is directed to the person of the supplicant, something I have never heard in witchcraft rites. But in its simple and direct way, it seems to me like a model for a prayer for those worshiping in the pagan way when no one can help them perform a ritual, when they cannot take part in a coven meeting, or perhaps just because they prefer to do it alone.

Here it is:

"A self-blessing—the pagan way.
"This ritual is best performed at the New Moon, but it may be done at other times. Need, not time of month, determines the performance. There is real power in the self-blessing, it should be used in time of need, and not done promiscuously.

"The purpose of the ritual is to bring the individual closer to the Godhead. It can also be used as a minor dedication or as a minor exorcism. It may be performed by any person upon themselves, at their will.

"Perform the ritual in a quiet place, free from distractions, and where the individual involved will not be disturbed. The ritual is to be done entirely nude. The required materials are:

"Salt—about a teaspoon is plenty.

"Wine—say an ounce.

"Water—about half as much as wine.

"Candle—votive or other.

"When you are ready to begin, sprinkle the salt on the floor and stand on it. Then you may light the candle. Mix the water into the wine and meditate upon your reasons for performing the self-blessing. At this point you are ready to begin. The indicated lines are to be said aloud.

"'Bless me, Mother, for I am thy child.'
"Dip the fingers of your right hand into the wine and water mixture and anoint your eyes:
"'Blessed be my eyes, that I may see thy path.'
"Anoint your nose:
"'Blessed be my nose, that I may breathe thy essence.'
"Anoint your mouth:
"'Blessed be my mouth, that I may speak of thee.'
"Anoint your breasts (females) arms (males):
"'Blessed be my breasts (arms), that I may be fruitful (strong) in my works.'
"Anoint your genitals:
"'Blessed be my genitals, which bring forth the life of man, as thou brought forth all creation.'
"Anoint your feet:
"'Blessed be my feet, that I may walk in thy way.'

"The result of this ritual is a feeling of peace, calm, and closeness to the Godhead. It is desirable that the participants bask in the afterglow so they may meditate and understand that they have called the attention of the Godhead to themselves, asking that they become more attuned to the Godhead.

"In cleaning up, let the candle burn out by itself. You may drink most of the wine left but leave enough to pour out upon the earth as a libation to the Mother."

*

Everywhere in the world the heirs of Wicca, whether or not they use that designation, carry on in the old ways. Even in Soviet Russia witchcraft is far from extinct. A recent story from Moscow, published in the *Los Angeles Times*, deals with the accusations of witchcraft and the subsequent turmoil in a Russian village called Borodenki, near Moscow. A few years ago the very thought of occult powers would have brought the Communist Party apparatus down on the villagers, and anyone suspected of psychic abilities, or any person practicing magic rituals, would surely have been dealt with by the authorities. But today even Russia accepts such matters without alarm. A commission was sent to the village to investigate the strange occurrences. In due time, the commission assured Moscow that it was all just silly superstition and nothing to worry about.

What the heirs of Wicca have inherited from the past may not always be the full wealth of wisdom and ritual as it once existed. But even part of that knowledge, imperfect though it may seem to some by comparison with the days of the Old Religion, is worth preserving. Whether one calls it being in tune with nature, anagnorisis, or kundalini—there are many roads leading toward it—there is only one ultimate goal.

BOOK TWO

OF WARLOCKS AND DEVILS AND DEMONS THAT COME IN THE NIGHT

Now that it is no longer illegal to worship the devil, those peculiar people among us who do so have acquired a kind of hero image in the eyes of those who would certainly never imitate them, but who would nevertheless like to know more about their activities. Even the press seems to have become preoccupied with the subject of the satanist revival movement.

Martha Robinet, a feature editor on the *Philadelphia Bulletin*, contacted me recently with a request to put her in touch with the nearest satanic group in her area. She hastened to add that this was strictly for publication purposes; she was interested in satanic gatherings and Black Masses only from a professional point of view. She said she realized, of course, that getting the story might involve some undercover work, but this would not bother her since she was a mature woman and a long-time newshound. She admitted that she had exhausted every source she could think of to get introduction to a satanic group and had come to me as a sort of last resort since I knew witches, ghosts, and such things and therefore that kind of contact was certainly in my area of interest.

Since her letter was written earnestly and certainly sincerely, I called Miss Robinet and explained how naïve her position really was. Groups worshiping the negative aspects of paganism are not particularly interested in publicity. They're happy to be left alone. There is also a tiny segment of people who use satanic concepts for private thrills, even crimes, and there is always the danger that a well-meaning reporter might stumble onto such a group and be a victim. While I do not by a long shot consider any of the satanists in this country or abroad to be depraved murderers or even the slightest bit dangerous, except perhaps to some minds for whom the satanic concept is not meant, I do know that satanism has occasionally been used as a front, a cover, for far more sinister activities. I don't think that the newshound from the *Philadelphia Bulletin* would have had time enough to find out which witch is which.

Those who do not know about Wicca, especially the uninformed press, like to refer to a male follower of witchcraft as a *warlock*. While the term "warlock" is certainly a valid description of a person engaged in pagan rituals, it is never used in Wicca, or 'white' witchcraft. A warlock is a man practicing some form of magic, generally in the nature of conjuration. The difference is quite obvious. Female and male witches worship the Mother Goddess Diana, and dedicate themselves to the principles of the Old Religion. They work healing spells or partake of other community enterprises. This kind of witchcraft is strongly religious in orientation, and the coven is more important than the individual. A warlock, on the other hand, is usually a solitary practitioner of whatever black or white arts he has managed to master. He is not concerned with any particular religious philosophy. If he works any spells, it is generally to help or hurt someone, not because he wishes to please any particular deity. Perhaps the modern term "magician" comes closest to what a medieval warlock was, except that the prestidigitator of today uses tricks and sleight-of-hand skills to produce his effects, while the warlock relies only on his superior knowledge of the laws of nature, his ability to manipulate them, and the powers within himself.

An American example of a practicing warlock is Theodore J. Rabouin. In his late thirties, Mr. Rabouin lives in Westborough, Massachusetts, and has been a practitioner of his craft for about seven years. Mr. Rabouin explains that he was the seventh son of a seventh son, as was his grandfather before him, and he attaches great significance to this fact. Furthermore, two of his great-great-great-grandfathers were executed for practicing witchcraft in Canada and France, so Mr. Rabouin considers himself a kind of hereditary warlock. Early in life, he became obsessed with the study of the occult. He grew up in a house directly across the street from a cemetery in Worcester, Massachusetts, and played among the graves the way other children play in streets. He is mainly self-educated because, as he puts it, he was too preoccupied with what is on the other side of the grave to worry about formal education.

At sixteen he took a job in the pathology department of a local hospital and found an eerie fascination in being among corpses. By age seventeen, he was in charge of the morgue. When not occupied at the hospital, he would spend his free time at the Worcester Museum of Natural History looking at stuffed animals, or endearing himself to the curators at the Worcester Art Museum so that they would let him handle some of the properties, like skulls. It never occurred to him that his preoccupation with death was anything but natural. Instead of dating as a teenager, he preferred to read about vampires, werewolves, and other such creatures.

Today, Mr. Rabouin is an aide at a local hospital working closely with psychiatrist M. Greenberg. He is not content with merely being a warlock but has engaged in various psychic activities as well such as an attempt to exorcise ghosts or using his own ESP powers to help people. By his own admission, his

involvement in the occult has rendered him more and more
unworldly.

*

Michael Howard is an intense young man in his early twenties
who makes a living as a gardener and part-time journalist. He
lives not far from London, England, and holds dim views of
traditional Wicca practitioners. According to the young man,
the Gardnerian witches are not real witches, and the Druidic
witches I met have nothing to do with genuine witchcraft.
He, on the other hand, being of the medieval tradition, more
closely represents the true image of what he considers a more
valid paganism. Mr. Howard worships, among others, the
"goat-foot god of ceremonial magic," the same deity the Greeks
called Pan, and he makes clear he worships the forces behind
the symbol, not the symbol itself. His worship of the goat-god
is purely metaphysical and based upon the idea that all gods
are one and that this is the creative force manifest throughout
nature. Above all, Mr. Howard does not think of himself as a
witch, but rather as a pagan following in a tradition directly
derived from the Knights Templars and through them from
ancient Egypt.

Neither witchcraft in the traditional sense, nor satanism, nor
even magic as practiced by warlocks is the "bag," as we would
call it today, of the Process. This religious movement calls itself the Church of the Final Judgement, and it has chapters
in Chicago, Boston, and elsewhere. The Chicago Chapter's
building, I hear, just burned down. I have no idea whether
there's any connection between the fire and the final judgment,
but the Process uses Christian symbols. Its priests are black-
robed, and communion services and sacraments are part of
the movement. This cult believes in three great gods of the
universe: Jehovah, Lucifer, and Satan. To them, these three
gods represent the basic human patterns, although there are
countless variations of those patterns just as there are countless
types of personalities.

All three of these gods, according to the Process, exist within all of us. Jehovah is the wrathful god of vengeance and retribution and demands discipline, courage, and ruthlessness. Lucifer, the light-bearer, urges us to enjoy life to the fullest, to look out for success, and to appreciate love, peace, and harmony one with the other. If this surprises you, my dear reader, the Process is quick in pointing out that Lucifer has mistakenly been identified with Satan. In this they are correct, by the way. Lucifer does mean "bearer of light," and in ancient Greece he was the brother of Diana, the moon goddess, and represented the sun. He is not to be confused with the fallen angel Lucifer, a Church-made symbol of early dissent.

In the Church of the Final Judgement, Christ and Satan are no longer enemies. They have found each other through love. Christ is the judge, and Satan executes Christ's judgment. The result is either salvation or doom. Satan, of course, has been greatly misunderstood by humanity—maligned, in fact, and anyone joining the Process would soon realize that the real image of Satan is not that commonly known. During the Sabbath assembly candles are lit, chants are sung, incense is burned, and both the Christian cross and the goat, symbol of Satan, adorn the altar.

The idea of this movement is to combine the powers of intellect and emotion to save the world. Applicants for membership are called acolytes. A member of the lowest rank in the Process hierarchy, an acolyte is first taught to sing special hymns. He then becomes the Processian, a member of the church who believes in the unity of Christ and Satan. "As you give, so shall you receive" is one of the tenets of this strange religion, and giving to the Process is not an act of helping someone, but merely an invitation to receive something in return. They don't care so long as the results are beneficial for both parties.

Only a week after becoming an acolyte, an applicant might very well become an initiate and be given the cross to signify his acceptance into the order. Six weeks later, he is ready to be baptized, to be given a new name, and to be accepted "into the unity of Christ and Satan as a Messenger of that unity."

To the Process, the idea of being born again means to have complete faith in the higher powers and not to worry about worldly matters. Worldly success brings nothing but transitory pleasure, and to know what one is and what one is to do in this world is far more important. If the world is in a sorry state, blame not God, but mankind.

But with all these lofty and spiritually tinged phrases, the Process is but another variation in the seemingly unending chain of bizarre religious movements.

*

Most churches consider sexual and other sensual indulgence a sure sign of the devil. Complete freedom to enjoy the gift of nature within oneself in conjunction with others is so powerful an instrument of fulfillment that to give it freely to everyone would deprive the religious establishment of its most potent weapons: constraint, reward, threat of sin, and above all, guilt.

Advocates of complete freedom in these areas point out the need of adjusting the social and moral scale, but in so doing they go to the other extreme. When everybody is equal, no one is anything. When sexual indulgence is no longer special in individuals, it will lose its attractiveness. Then, too, such extremist movements tend to attract undesirables and maladjusted people who would quite naturally endanger what limited validity there might be in the extreme philosophy.

When such extremist groups join with other pagan groups in overall organizations, they tend to embarrass the more seriously orientated movements.

Such has been the case recently with the Psychedelic Venus Church of San Francisco. Although still a member of the Council of Themis, the umbrella organization covering several pagan groups in California, there has been increasing disenchantment among the leaders of the Council of Themis with the activities of the Psychedelic Venus Church. It is not so much the actual physical activities of the Venus Church that are being condemned, but the motivating factors and the lack of the spiritual element, which alone can make sensual freedoms acceptable. Orgies for their own sake are meaningless. The orgies of the ancient Dionysian festivals had not only a deeply religious purpose, but served to unleash creative forces within the participants and to stir up the power within them. The resultant power was then used for the benefit of the community, whether on an individual or a collective basis. The Dionysian orgy was never its own reward.

Not so with the Psychedelic Venus Church, which has several hundred members and is headquartered in Berkeley, California. The main sacraments are sex and marijuana smoking, and the newsletter of the organization is called *Intercourse*. *Intercourse* stresses that pot is preferred as a sacramental, but that other stimulants, even wine, are also acceptable. The newsletter advises against the use of LSD, commenting that the worshipers of the Indian Siva, their "parent religion," prefer "gentle grass."

The guiding spirit, if that's the phrase, of this group is Jefferson Poland, and his main purpose seems to be to help the American sexual revolution along in whatever way he can. According to the *Los Angeles Free Press* of March 13, 1970, the church membership includes women, homosexual males, and heterosexual males. While sex has always played some part in pagan religions, it is usually reserved for the highest rituals and restricted to initiates. Then, too, its main purposes in other pagan cults is to create psychic energies for specific purposes. In the Psychedelic Venus Church, however, no specific purposes are necessary. According to the *Los Angeles Free Press*, the rituals of the "pot sex church" are their own reward. One version of the holy sacrament, the genital sacrifice, is performed four times a year at witches' Sabbaths. In this celebration, the congregation lies down nude, and one person of each sex offers himself on the altar. The genitals of these two volunteers are thickly spread with honey, and one by one the worshipers come up to the altar and lick the honey off the sex organs of the two volunteers.

According to Jefferson Poland, who has a minister's certificate from the State of California for his "church," this is a ritual of very ancient origin, and he compares it to the Christian communion in which worshipers partake of the flesh and blood of Christ. I doubt that many Christians will agree with this version of the sacrament.

*

Do people really believe in the devil?

Miss M.J.M., a young woman living in Ohio, is convinced that a curse has been placed upon her. Her father, now dead, allegedly practiced black magic. How does Miss M. know all this? Why, her life has been a total mess. Nothing works right, she is unhappy all of the time, so there surely must be a curse in operation.

David G. of Seattle, Washington, wonders if it is possible to prolong life through witchcraft. He knows that strange things can be accomplished ever since he met a demon in the spring of 1960 who called himself the "Satan of destruction."

M.W. of Virginia isn't sure whether she is psychic, mad, or possessed by the devil. It all started when she tried to contact her recently deceased mother with a ouija board. Soon after that, she began to hear voices when there was no one around. She decided to see a priest and informed him that she thought herself possessed by the devil. Soon after she was put into a hospital, but the voices continued, and she found herself in a state bordering on trance in which she could see and hear her loved ones yet was unable to move. She is rational enough to understand the meaning of psychic phenomena and realizes that the voices she hears may be those of discarnates.

She assures me that she has contacted the devil and describes him as looking like a dirty goat from the waist down. He stood straight up in front of her, but when he moved, he seemed to be like someone walking on stilts. Thanks to her acquaintance with the devil, she also knows that just before you enter hell, there are a lot of large, dark rocks. Her soul apparently stayed on one of these rocks until an angel came to rescue her. They look like granite, and there is a solid rock tunnel reaching straight into hell itself. Then, as you enter, there is a lake on the right, and it is here that you encounter a dog with a human head. Hell is filled with a thick black fog and there is neither sun, moon, nor sky. Whenever she stood in line for communion, the devil, she explained, cursed her. I advised the lady to send the devil packing and to stop using the ouija board.

*

When it comes to the nearest thing to a real Satan in the United States, we must all turn towards the smiling countenance of Anton Szandor LaVey, erstwhile lion tamer, police photographer, amateur painter, amateur organist, the man who played the devil in the motion picture *Rosemary's Baby*, and nowadays engaged, profitably, I hope, as the chief executive officer of the Church of Satan in San Francisco. I have written of LaVey and his rituals in *The Truth About Witchcraft*. Mr. LaVey gives his disciples a formidable service. It is staged properly, there are sound effects, his satanic bible is a well-written and effective manual, and Mr. LaVey himself, shaven head and goatee and all that, is the very image of a modern devil.

Anton LaVey believes that his satanic religion caters to the selfishness, the need for self-indulgence, and the lust within many of us. He doesn't advocate murder, destruction, Black Masses, or any formal defiance of other religions. His Church of Satan is a fun-type cult using all the clichés and props of the devil worshiper but none of the more permanent effects such as murder, sacrifice, or inverted ritual. Defilement of God does exist in some satanist groups, especially in England, but LaVey is satisfied to praise Satan. Let God take care of himself. I cannot guarantee that you won't lose your soul if you attend one of Anton LaVey's rites at his black-painted church on California Street in San Francisco, but you're not in any mortal danger, nor are you entering a den of crime.

However, LaVey and friends can be somewhat miffed if others try to steal their thunder.

*

In December 1970, my good friend Virginia Cameron, director of the Cincinnati Parapsychology Forum, sent me a long article from the *Cincinnati Inquirer* dealing with a Satanic church that had just opened shop in staid Cincinnati. CITY INTRODUCED TO DEVIL WORSHIP, the headline said, and Ben Kaufman, the *Inquirer*'s religion reporter, wrote: "The worship of Satan has a foothold in Cincinnati with the establishment of a church dedicated to that fallen angel." (Mr. Kaufman evidently did not know that Lucifer was the fallen angel, or if he did, he didn't care *who* fell.) "Unlike the notorious West Coast churches of Satan, this one is devoid of sexual activity."

To begin with, there is only one West Coast Church of Satan, the aforementioned San Francisco one, and there are no sexual activities as part of the service since satanists believe sex to be such an ordinary and normal part of life that to emphasize it would be ludicrous. Other than a living altar of flesh, the naked body of a woman serving as the altar, sexual activities in the satanic movement are restricted to certain rare fertility rites, and then only on special occasions privately conducted between consenting adults.

The Cincinnati version of devil worship is the brainchild of James and Linda Guthrie, who love performing rituals in the black-painted sanctuary in the basement of their home. Mr. Guthrie is a salesman and his wife a professional dancer. The couple have created all their ritual objects and props except for the skulls, daggers, black candles, and incense burners.

Evidently the Guthries have their own version of satanism.

According to the *Cincinnati Inquirer*, part of the initiation is to claim, "I deny God the Creator of heaven and earth." With the help of Satan, the Cincinnati priest claims, one can obtain power, and with power one can make things happen in one's life. Black Masses, props such as a cross hung upside down, and the Lord's Prayer being said backward are also part of Mr. Guthrie's cult. In this respect he differs greatly from Anton LaVey's church. Mr. LaVey, in fact, differs a great deal with Mr. Guthrie.

As soon as the rather lengthy article had appeared in the *Cincinnati Inquirer*, a letter from San Francisco arrived at the newspaper office, which the *Inquirer*, ever aware of reader interest in the occult, printed immediately. Through a spokesman, the Reverend Lawrence Green, the Church of Satan of San Francisco took vigorous exception to the Satan-come-lately establishment in the Queen City. There is only one Church of Satan in existence and it is located in San Francisco, explained the Reverend Green, taking great pains to point out that the names Church of Satan, First Church of Satan, First Church of Satan in America and Satanic Church are all legally protected. Happily, Reverend Green continued, he understood that the people of Cincinnati had refused to accept "this villainy in their midst," and he made it plain that the San Francisco Church of Satan would have no truck with those Cincinnati upstarts. The statement also referred to "gross misconceptions related to our religion," very likely referring to the inclusion of Black Mass practices, which, however, left those domiciled in the Cincinnati area and wishing to become satanists without a proper church to turn to.

It turned out that matters were even worse. Even those among the Queen City population who had been willing to accept the Guthrie version of the devilish gospel, despite the satanic rebuff from Anton LaVey, were deprived of this opportunity two months later. Twenty-two-year-old James Guthrie announced that he was leaving town with his congregation.

He was going to assume his priestly duties at a Hollywood Boulevard Church of Satan in Los Angeles and to become curator of the church's new "weird museum" next door. What had made things come to a head was not only a complaint from the Society for the Prevention of Cruelty to Animals about slaughtering animals for sacrifice, but also a ruling by the Building Department of the city declaring Mr. Guthrie's basement unsuitable for services. He had also lost his job. Anyone who says any publicity is good publicity isn't a satanist!

*

But wait. There is such a thing as a good satanist. His name is Dr. Herbert Sloane, a man in his sunny years, a professional cardopractor (card reader) and former barber who gives tarot readings to those wishing to be told of their future. Herb Sloane has the personality and appearance of a vaudevillian of old. He is a gentle, kind person full of humor and compassion for his fellow man. He is a widely traveled man, in the middle west that is, and he has more friends in his home town of Toledo, Ohio, than some churchmen have in all of the United States. I had corresponded with Herb for about three years before I finally met him, for the opportunity to visit Toledo, Ohio, does not come very often.

Herb's strange religious convictions came to him in 1908. Although he is friendly toward all witches, he worships the Lord Sathanas. He is a witch of the Ophitic Gnostic Sect, and Herb has had that strange religion for sixty-three of his sixty-six years. Time doesn't mean a great deal in the life of Herb Sloane. For over thirty years he has been trying to get to New York City but has never quite made it; yet he never stops hoping that some day he *will*. The Great White Way still holds romantic attraction for him. When you live in Toledo, Ohio, the big city does seem kind of glamorous. But Herb does most of his traveling through the mail. His modest quarters and office in back of the barbershop in one of Toledo's quieter business districts is filled with devilish paraphernalia in accordance with his professed religion. The front of the railroad flat is his former barbershop. Here the walls are covered with photographs of famous people who have sat in his chair at one time or another, and for some reason, well-endowed young females, not too over-dressed, are more in evidence than staid old men. But that is as it should be, for surely the Lord Sathanas must have had a wife or at least a girl friend.

Herb has had his fair share of publicity in such diverse publications as *Fate* magazine and the *National Enquirer*. He's got the gift of gab and makes a good guest on some of the local talk shows. When he heard that I was doing another book on the pagan religions, he offered me what in political life is called "the key to the city." Aware of my having been through many initiations in various forms of witchcraft, he considered me an insider and invited me to one of the Sabbaths.

Witchcraft in Toledo is practiced mainly by two individuals, Herb Sloane and his satanic group, and a charming lady by the name of Jeffery Cather. Mrs. Cather runs a boutique of the unusual called Circe's Treasures. Here she sells anything from standard occult items to homemade candles, which are very beautiful and unusual, but she does not sell initiations or rituals, as far as I can determine. Her witchcraft, it would appear, is her private affair. According to Herb Sloane, she is a fourth-generation hereditary witch and apparently Toledo is big enough for the two of them.

Since the local chapter of the Association for Research and Enlightenment, also known as the Cayce Foundation, had asked me to lecture for them in Toledo, I decided to combine my visit with attendance at one of Herb Sloane's Sabbaths.

Herb figured out that on October 14 the moon would be full and it would be a perfect time for me to attend the celebration of the Our Lady of Endor Coven of the Ophite Gnostic Cultus Sathanas. Ophitic Gnostics celebrate two high holidays, or esbats, of a thirteen-moon year, Sathanasmas on October 31, and Lilithmas on April 30. New Year's Day falls on November

1. In this coven, the days begin at sunrise rather than at midnight as is the custom with the Christian calendar or at sundown as with the Jews. Herb granted me the greatest privilege of them all: if by any chance the full moon wasn't satisfactory because of travel commitments, he would call a *special* Sabbath in my honor. (Incidentally, his group requires no formal membership, no dues or collections, with good fellowship [and girlship] the sole bond holding them together as far as the earthly structure is concerned. As far as the spiritual edifice goes, Herb explained, Lord Sathanas himself was holding that together.) I asked if I might shoot some scenes for my documentary film dealing with pagan religions and offered to pay a nominal sum in return for the customary release papers. Happily, Herb acceded to my request, but he refused any financial consideration.

On September 1, Herb Sloane informed me that it was Lord Sathanas himself who had a major role in arranging my schedule so that I could be with them on October 14. I would be initiated into the group at the same time, as that was part of this special visit. Herb added, "In gnostic parlance we would say you were called rather than initiated, and it is no one less than Our Lord Himself who in our cult does the initiation or extends the call and not the coven leader."

A week later, Herb brought me up to date on what to expect on my Toledo visit. Proceedings would be held in the Dragon Room, which also doubles as Herb's living quarters and their covenstead. One of his favorite witches, whom he called his "left-hand witch Huldah," would not be present since she was in the hospital. Herb asked me to pay her a visit, which I did, and the lady turned out to be a charming person, optimistic despite her serious illness. As for the Dragon Room, it looked best in semidarkness. With candles flickering, the "icons" (as Herb called the various pictures, photographs, and designs on the walls) looked rather impressive and gave the small elongated room the feeling of a secret hiding place. Not the least of the items on the walls was a brass devil's mask mounted on a black plate, which I had brought with me as a gift to Lord Sathanas' favorite Toledo priest. There were also a small doll which played a certain part in the proceedings, as I was to learn later, and for some reason the large framed picture of a lady wrestler. The altar was very simple, devil's mask and all, and it was clear that Dr. Sloane did not practice his unusual religion for material gain.

It seemed particularly refreshing to hear Herb Sloane explain the modesty of their service in ways which made the negative seem rather like an asset. There would be no wine for the communion; instead the coven used apple juice. This, Herb explained, was symbolical of the apple their Lord Sathanas used to seduce the Blessed Mother Eve in Eden. According to their theology, that was the first gnosis, a word roughly meaning enlightenment. Herb also informed me that he expected me to deliver a short sermon during the Sabbath. Now I have delivered speeches before skeptical women's clubs, sleepy salesmen, and rebellious students, and never had any difficulty with any of them, so I did not expect to be nonplussed by a coven of devil worshipers.

Herb had been kind enough to arrange for a room at the Hotel Commodore Perry downtown and to notify the illustrious Toledo newspaper the *Blade* of my arrival. Shortly after I had gotten into town, an attractive young lady named Carole Williams and a staff photographer appeared in my room, not through materialization but through the door. The result was a seven-column article in the *Toledo Blade,* in which my witch-hunting activities—that was the local joke—were explained in great detail, or as far as one can in a Midwestern family newspaper. Step by step, Herb Sloane had prepared me for the momentous occasion to come. He next sent me a typed "order of service." It reads as follows: "Our Lady of Endor Coven, the Ophitic Gnostic Cultus Sathanas. Doctor H. Sloane covenator. The call. The invocation. The creed. First reading. Announcements. Supplication. Communion. Second reading. Sermon. Benediction. Social hour."

The big night had arrived. After a sumptuous Hungarian-style dinner at the home of Mr. and Mrs. R. A. Matuszak, leaders of the local Cayce Foundation chapter, and a truly inspiring lecture on reincarnation at the library auditorium, I said good night to my hosts and in the company of radio announcer Bill Gill proceeded to the Dragon Room. Bill, an ordained Unitarian minister as well as a broadcaster, was a friend of Herb Sloane's and just as welcome as I was. Awaiting us were five other people besides Sloane. These were two men and three women, mostly in their twenties and thirties, with the ladies professing to be witches while the men allowed that they were *interested* in coven activities of this particular type. With one exception, they were all members in good standing of Sloane's little group. When the hour of nine had struck, everybody donned his robe and hood and seated himself along the wall facing the "covenator," who stood at the rostrum with his back to the altar. Bill Gill and I seated ourselves on the bed which took up a corner near the entrance to the room. I was going to record the sound of the service during the actual Sabbath and film a little of it afterward.

Herb Sloane disappeared for a moment to get ready for the action. When he returned he wore a black cape, and his impressive face was now crowned by two plastic horns, securely stuck onto his forehead. After a moment of hushed silence, in which the subdued sound of the motor in my tape recorder was the only noise heard, Herb Sloane took a deep breath and began the service by ringing a bell. Addressing himself first to Bill and me and then to the congregation, his voice steady and clear, he sounded a lot like any Methodist or Baptist minister or perhaps even the head of the Kiwanis Club—except, of course, for those horns.

*

"Our Lady of Endor Coven of the Ophitic Gnostic Cult of Sathanas is now in Sabbath, and this will be the order of service: the call, which you've just heard, the invocation, the creed, first reading, announcements, supplication, communion, second reading, sermon, benediction, and social hour. Let's bow our heads for the invocation. Lord Sathanas, we invoke into this covenstead thy sacred presence this Sabbathnight, that thou be with us in understanding, that thou open our ears to hear and understand the things which we should understand, and close our ears and minds to those things which are not pleasing to thee. Thank you, Lord. Nema, Nema, Nema, Nema! Now repeat after me. I believe in an infinite intelligence—"

THE PEOPLE: "*I believe in an infinite intelligence—*"

"—incomprehensible to all finite beings—"

"*—incomprehensible to all finite beings—*"

"I believe in Sathanas as my Savior—"

"*I believe in Sathanas as my Savior—*"

"—by virtue of the Ophitic gnosis—"

"*—by virtue of the Ophitic gnosis—*"

"—booned by him to our Blessed Mother Eve in the garden of Eden."

"*—booned by him to our Blessed Mother Eve in the garden of Eden.*"

"I believe in Eve as our mundane mother—"

"*I believe in Eve as our mundane mother—*"

"—the blessed Lillith as our spiritual mother."

"*—the blessed Lillith as our spiritual mother.*"

"I believe in Asmodius—"

"*I believe in Asmodius—*"

"—and all the powers and principalities of the celestial realms of Sathanas."

"*—and all the powers and principalities of the celestial realms of Sathanas.*"

"I believe in the communion of the succubus and the incubus."

"*I believe in the communion of the succubus and the incubus.*"

"I believe in the gnosis of the Ophitic coven of Sathanas—"

"*I believe in the gnosis of the Ophitic coven of Sathanas—*"
"—in magic—"
"*—in magic—*"
"—and in final release—"
"*—and in final release—*"
"—of the souls of all faithful witches—"
"*—of the souls of all faithful witches—*"
"—from the powers of disdained demiurge—"
"*—from the powers of disdained demiurge—*"
"—unto a life everlasting in Orkus."
"*—unto a life everlasting in Orkus.*"
"All this through the power—"
"*All this through the power—*"
"—the goodness—"
"*—the goodness—*"
"—the guidance and wisdom—"
"*—the guidance and wisdom—*"
"—of our Lord Sathanas—"
"*—of our Lord Sathanas—*"
"—worlds without end—"
"*—worlds without end—*"
"Nema."
"*Nema.*"
"Nema."
"*Nema.*"
"*Nema.*"
"Nema."
"*Nema.*"

Taking a deep breath and pausing momentarily, Herb Sloane then continued:

"Let us turn to the first reading of the Sabbath, and let me beg the pardon of some of you that have been so long and so regular in attendance. But again I am using as the first reading that reading that I have so oft used before. But I feel it has

a place in this Sabbath, and hence I've taken the liberty of
using it. Not that I don't value it as very highly, but I just
don't want you to think that I'm using it too often. I want
to read from *The Gnostic Religions*, by Hans Jonas, the very
roots of our religion. 'Now in the same oppositional vein was
the gnostic view of the serpent, and its role in inducing Eve
to eat of the tree. For more than one reason, not the least of
which was the mention of knowledge, the biblical tale exerts
a strong attraction upon agnostics. Since it is the serpent that
persuades Adam and Eve to taste of the fruit of knowledge and
thereby to disobey their Creator, it came on a whole group of
systems to represent the thematic principle from Beyond, coun-
teracting the designs of the demiurge, and thus could become
as much a symbol of the power of redemption as a biblical
god had been degraded to a symbol of cosmic oppression.

" 'Indeed, more than one gnostic sect derives its name from
the cult of the serpent: ophite, from the Greek *ophs*; naceans,
from the Hebrew *nachas*, the group as a whole being termed
ophitic and this position of the serpent is based on the biblical
text. This is the version found in the ophitic psalter of Aranus.
The transmundane mother, Sophia Pinokis, tries to counteract
the demiurgic activity of her apostatic son, Ealgabeo, sends the
serpent to seduce Adam and Eve into breaking Ealgabeo's commands. The plan succeeds. Both eat of the tree, of which God,
the demiurge, had forbidden them to eat. But when they had
eaten, they knew the power from beyond and turned away from
the Creator. It is the first success of the transcendental principle
against the principle of the world, which is vitally interested in
preventing knowledge in man as the interworldly hostage of
light. The serpent's action marks the beginning of all gnosis
on earth, which thus by its very origins is stamped as opposed
to the world and its god, and, indeed, as a form of rebellion.'
Thus endeth the first reading of the Sabbath."

With all the eloquence of a preelection toastmaster at a
banquet, Herb Sloane then introduced me to his little group,

after which Bill Gill got the guest treatment. This was followed by announcements of Herb Sloane's various appearances
in person and on radio or television. He was particularly proud
to announce that he would be at Whitmore High School three
days before Hallowe'en for both a morning and an afternoon
lecture, under the auspices of the Department of English.
Next came the two gifts I had brought him, which he seemed
genuinely to enjoy. The brass devil's head on a black plate
mounted above the altar looked as if it had always been in
place, nicely highlighted by the two candles underneath. In
addition, I had ceremoniously put a necklace and amulet around
his neck. It was one of the necklaces designed and made by
my good friend Sára Cunningham of Pasadena, California, not
an ophitic witch but a witch nevertheless. After this, Herb
asked all present to send healing thoughts to the lady in the
hospital. Hands were joined and in a moment of silence, with
heads bowed, we all sent forth hopes of speedy recovery to the
absent member of the group. Then the covenator continued
with the proceedings:

"We'll now have the supplication for all the benefactors of
the coven, and for the souls of the faithful departed.

"And let us make this supplication in a manner like we did
the Credo. Salutations, O Sathanas, who art in Orkus."

THE PEOPLE: *"Salutations, O Sathanas, who art in Orkus."*
"We of this coven hallow thy name."
"We of this coven hallow thy name."
"Let ever thy powers and principalities come—"
"Let ever thy powers and principalities come—"
"—that thy will may be made manifest—"
"—that thy will may be made manifest—"
"—among thy faithful witches in this mundane sphere—"
"—among thy faithful witches in this mundane sphere—"
"—even as it is in Orkus."
"—even as it is in Orkus."

"Give us this moon the guidance of Asmodius in our vocations."

"Give us this moon the guidance of Asmodius in our vocations."

"Salutations, O Lord."

"Salutations, O Lord."

"Help us in our enchantments."

"Help us in our enchantments."

"Sathanas—"

"Sathanas—"

"—inspire our souls to demonstrate gratitude—"

"—inspire our souls to demonstrate gratitude—"

"—as the highest of thy directives."

"—as the highest of thy directives."

"Allow us not to fall into demiurgic paths—"

"Allow us not to fall into demiurgic paths—"

"—but keep us ever under the mystical shadow of thy trident."

"—but keep us ever under the mystical shadow of thy trident."

"Hail, Eve, full of wisdom."

"Hail, Eve, full of wisdom."

"Blessed art thou amongst witches."

"Blessed art thou amongst witches."

"And blessed is the fruit of thy womb, Cain."

"And blessed is the fruit of thy womb, Cain."

"Hallowed Mother Eve—"

"Hallowed Mother Eve—"

"—receiver of the gnosis—"

"—receiver of the gnosis—"

"—most gracious Mother Eve—"

"—most gracious Mother Eve—"

"—grandmother of Enoch—"

"—grandmother of Enoch—"

"—petition for us now—"

"*—petition for us now—*"
"—and at the hour of our disincarnations."
"*—and at the hour of our disincarnations.*"
"So be it now and forever more—"
"*So be it now and forever more—*"
"—worlds without end."
"*—worlds without end.*"

"Nema, Nema, Nema, Nema. The hallowed part of our Sabbath, the memorial to our blessed Lord Sathanas, when we take communion symbolic of the first gnosis, which was in our first reading of this Sabbath. I will go counterclockwise with this chalice, and you will stand to take communion."

After everyone had taken a sip of apple cider from the chalice, Herb returned to his pulpit. The covenator decided to have a second reading from one of the books that mention his work, after which I was asked to come forward and address the coven. Without hesitation, I stood up and told them how important it was that they pursue their own way toward the deity, whatever the deity's name might be. It wasn't much of a speech, as my lectures go, but it seemed to hit just the right tone, for everyone listened attentively. I then turned the meeting back to Herb, who for the benefit of myself and Bill Gill explained once again why the life-size doll was still sitting on the bed. April Belle, as he called her, wasn't just a toy. He had read about a similar life-size doll in a book some years before and become so obsessed with the idea of owning such a doll that he got a friend in Cleveland to make him one. As time went on, he became convinced that there was telepathy between April Belle and himself.

As early as 1930, Herb Sloane had decided to be a coven priest, although at that time he had no coven and was more of a missionary in the cause of Lord Sathanas than someone with his own community. But when the doll joined him in 1946, it seems, things fell into place. She has even "materialized" for Herb through a local medium, sort of misty but clear enough for him to make her out. Melinda, one of his covenites, also noticed the manifestation. Herb Sloane credits April Belle with his present coven. He thinks it was the doll who brought them all together.

*

If all this seems a far cry from devil worshiping and evil practices, it is. Herb Sloane's Lord Sathanas doesn't seduce anyone. As a matter of fact, Lord Sathanas is rather reluctant to let anyone come near him. Unlike Anton LaVey's Church of Satan, which appeals directly to man's inborn lust and self-ishness and encourages the enjoyment of life *now* rather than preparing for a better hereafter, the Toledo satanists derive their position from the story of Adam and Eve. They simply do not accept the division of the world into a good force, God, and an evil force, Satan. To them, both forces are at least equal, al-though they prefer Satan. It is a little like a French Canadian opting for a French-language school even though he lives in a predominantly English-speaking country.

The articles of faith and the prayer at the end of the service are obviously patterned after similar prayers in the Christian religion. Nema, the prayer word at the end of an invocation, is simply amen spelled backward. Orkus is the opposite of heaven—the underworld, hell. The Demiurge is the Greek con-cept of the dominant, "good" deity, that which we commonly call the Creator. Of course, one might argue that the legend of the serpent and the seduction of Eve are symbolic of the discovery of sex. Almost all civilizations, at one time or an-other, have recognized the symbolism of the serpent as a cover-up for sexual activities. Asmodius, a demon also met in the Hebrew concept of hell, is frequently invoked by medieval kab-balists. Here he functions as a kind of second in command to the Lord Sathanas. Finally, Lillith is another aspect of the Moon Goddess, having to do with the dark side, the hidden, the occult. As the Hebrew and Christian traditions recognize

Abel as the preferred seed of the first couple, Adam and Eve, so the satanists look to Cain as their hero.

In a way, satanists do reverse Christian values, but this is not done to offend Christians or their religion; it is simply an insistence on the other side of the coin, following the left-hand path rather than the right-hand way. Since, in the satanists' view, both paths were orginally equal, neither being wholly good nor wholly bad, they do not view themselves as followers of an evil religion. There is nothing in this version of satanism that calls for action against other religions. There is no request for any evil acts, crimes, unnatural acts, or the forswearing of one's faith in some other cult or religion.

To the contrary, the creed is stated simply, without coercion, and without great promises. Compare this with some of the outrageous and unrealistic promises made by Establishment religions, Christian and otherwise, and the almost pathological threats against those following other paths, and it becomes clear that the satanists are not nearly as terrifying as the word might indicate. Especially not in Toledo, Ohio.

BOOK THREE

ISIS AND ISHTAR:
THE COMEBACK OF ANCIENT CULTS

"Velcome to the house of Ishtar," said a female voice in dulcet yet exciting tones. A slight Russian accent made it even more incongruous, for I was standing at the threshold of a modest house on a tree-shaded lane in Pasadena. The year was 1969, the season All Hallows' Eve and the occasion, my long-awaited visit to Feraferia, a unique coven of pagans worshiping in the ancient Greek traditions.

I looked up in the semidarkness and found that the voice belonged to a pretty, dark-haired woman dressed in the flowing robe of a priestess. The material was quite sheer and her pale skin showed through it. An elaborate necklace and headdress, amulets, bracelets, and anklets, all of which were of a kind I had never seen before, completed her costume. The house, an older, very comfortable building, set back somewhat from the quiet street, was ideally suited for a secret ritual. Although I was yet to learn that prying neighbors will always find a way to disrupt that which they cannot understand or participate in, at the time I first met the people of Feraferia all was serene and the night was quiet and warm.

I had originally heard of Fred Adams and his strange pagan

sect through a mutual friend, Mark Roberts of Dallas. After some correspondence with the president of Feraferia, Richard Stanewick, I was finally invited to their autumnal ritual. Both Fred and Richard are professional artists. Fred's mate, Svetlana, the lady who had so enticingly greeted me at the door, liked to create jewelry and strange designs, and everything in and about Feraferia, as I was soon to learn, was done by the people themselves in a unique manner based on authentic ancient models and ideas. Feraferia describes itself as "a love culture for wilderness" and ecological concepts were at the core of its teachings long before ecology became a household term in America, long before an alarmed country became finally aware of the need to preserve what is left of our natural heritage. Fred Adams lives and breathes preservation, return to the natural state of living, the planting of new trees, the saving of city areas from destruction, the cleansing and purification of rural areas. Those are as important to him and his group as are the more involved pagan rituals, worshiping the "magic maiden," the symbolic deity representing the female principle in nature, creation, the spark within.

Feraferia does not call itself witchcraft by that name. It is far more. Where Wicca or male-oriented witchcraft groups worship in rites to express their desires symbolically and, through incantations, try to change things for themselves or for others, Feraferia goes beyond the ritual: It enacts what it stands for in actual nature. There are side trips, weather permitting, into the wilderness, where the group communes with nature. There are attempts at restoring neglected areas to their natural appearance, and as a consequence, even the ritual is far more realistic and vital than the rituals of so many intellectually inclined pagan groups.

Promptly at seven-thirty, Richard had called for me at the Hotel Continental in Hollywood. The ride out to Pasadena takes about thirty or forty minutes. We talked very little en route. As we approached Pasadena, Richard said, "You know about our principles, don't you?" I nodded, I had done some reading beforehand and I was fully prepared to learn more firsthand. Of course, I didn't come to this group exactly as a novice. Fred knew that I had been through several high-level pagan initiations before and that I was probably familiar with the ancient Greek aspects of his group since I had originally been a classical archeologist. I didn't know, of course, to what degree I would be welcome tonight. After all, they knew I would write about the group, although I had promised not to disclose anything that would be in violation of their trust in me. There are certain words in all magic rituals that should not be disclosed to anyone other than an actual initiate hearing them for the first time. But there are other things, especially visual descriptions of certain rituals, that can be safely disclosed to outsiders, especially if the purpose is to explain a little-known cult and possibly interest others in studying it. "You have no hangups, do you?" Dick continued. "Some of our rites are done in the nude." I wasn't particularly surprised since most Wicca groups also worship in the nude. I had long learned that being naked did not necessarily mean misbehaving.

There were already six or seven people assembled in the living room of "the house of Ishtar." The lights were not too bright, but they were strong enough to disclose an incredible array of paraphernalia covering literally every inch of space along the walls. There were drawings, paintings, figurines, ritual objects, leaves, wreaths, small altars—much of it the work of Fred Adams himself. All of these objects fitted well together, and turned the room into a kind of outer temple. The inner temple, I was to learn later, was much smaller and quite different. Many of the art objects along the walls represented beautiful young women, since the "magic maiden" of this cult is a young girl about twenty-three years old rather than the Mother Goddess of slightly more mature connotations generally worshiped in other witchcraft cults.

Everything about Feraferia is vibrant and love-orientated.

Feraferia does not contain a negative ritual. While there are some protective incantations and spells in Wicca to ward off enemies or evil human beings, Feraferia has none of those. This group believes that the positive force alone will protect them. All ritualistic activity in Feraferia revolves around the ancient Greek calendar, based upon thirteen lunar months of twenty-eight days each. Every moment is carefully charted by Fred Adams in an elaborate and intricate calendar, which he himself has constructed. The inner secret of this pagan group is to be completely in tune with what goes on in nature, to find the right moment for whatever one is undertaking, the right auspices, and not merely a casual glance at the horoscope. This goes far deeper than any astrologer normally does. A rhythmical tying up with nature's own inner movements is the ultimate goal for the men and women in Feraferia. As a result, their lives become wholly attuned to natural living, bringing, Feraferia believes, total immersion, total fulfillment, and a way of life different from the city-bred destructiveness and ill health to which Fred and his friends ascribe so many of today's ills.

Except for the priestess, whose dress apparently required greater preparation, the others were still in their "civilian clothes." There were one couple from a nearby community, who were friends of Fred, a local doctor, a lady whom he had brought, a young girl with long dark hair who seemed to know everyone already, Fred, Dick, and myself. I was the only new person in this gathering. Altogether there were nine people, five men and four women. The room was heavy with incense, and the conversation flowed freely as these people exchanged greetings and brought each other up to date on their doings since the last time they had gathered together.

Promptly at nine o'clock, Fred asked for attention. "We are about ready to begin," he explained. "Ladies can change in the bedroom, gentlemen in the kitchen." Quickly the two sexes repaired to their respective changing quarters and a little later emerged wearing white robes. I had not brought any such garment, so Fred kindly lent me an extra one. The robes are kept in the temple and since some members of the group hadn't come tonight, there was a spare robe available.

After we had filed back into the living room, we were told to lie down on the floor, heads touching in starlike fashion and legs outward bound. As we gazed up at the ceiling, we were to try astralprojection together. Actually this was a kind of communal relaxation, in that for a few moments we would forget our worldly problems and try to relate to each other as parts of a larger community. I don't think I flew up to the ceiling and out the window the way I was directed, but I did experience a calm sense of relaxation and it was rather a warm feeling to rub ears with someone you had just met, yet without having any sensation of being close to a stranger.

This was followed by some yoga breathing exercises, which relaxed us even further. As we sat up on the floor on top of what turned out to be a carefully engraved calendar wheel, Fred stepped up to a small altar in the corner, where he was joined by Svetlana. In front of the effigy of the magic maiden, the female goddess Ishtar, or Astar, the priestly couple then intoned the proper ritual prayer requesting that the goddess be present in our undertaking.

To the left of the altar there was an icon of Kore, the Greek name for "the magic maiden" of wildness, while to the right was a similar picture honoring Kouros, her male counterpart, the "magic youth" of wildness. Between them was placed a picture or symbol of Awiya, also called Korythalia, the great tree of the cosmos. According to Feraferia interpretation, this tree is the seat of Sophia, whom Frederick Adams calls "the black goddess of unfathomable mystery, who unites Kore and Kouros in unending love, dance, play, dream fulfillment." In addition to these symbolic representations, to the east of the altar was a musical instrument representing air; to the south, an incense burner representing fire; a mortar and pestle with soil inside representing earth to the west; a container of water placed to the north; some pebbles in the center representing the omphalos—what Adams calls the "earth sky navel" of ritual significance—a bell to call the spirits of nature; and finally various talismans or charms on the ground in front of the altar to mark the four quarters.

A special ritual movement, almost a dance, was performed in front of the altar to open the proceedings. This movement is called phytala, and is enacted by first putting the palms of the hands together, then raising them above one's head, opening the arms wide, bringing them down toward the lower solar plexus, letting the arms hang loose by the sides of the body, and finally lifting them up, palms outward, in an attitude of blessing. During this posturing, a chant up and down the tonal scale is intoned: "Magic maiden, magic maiden, evoe Kore, evoe Kouros, Awiya." *Evoe* means "hail!" There is another chant in honor of Kore that may also be used on this as well as other occasions:

"O holy maiden of the kindling quick of merging mist and mazing echo, the innocent bounty of the trees bears your faerie flesh of wildness, wonder, magic, mirth, and love. Your beauty seals our bridal with all life. The dance of your green pulse unfolds all bodies from earth's fragrant form."

Evidently, everyone except me had been through such ceremonies before because they responded immediately with their own "Evoe Kore, evoe Kouros, Awiya! Hail, holy maiden, hail, holy youth, hail, great lady of living cosmos and of eternal wildness and love."

Now the priest motioned us to rise and follow him and the priestess out into the garden, where we would enact an outdoor ceremonial. One by one we walked through the rear door of the house, down a few steps into the rather large garden behind the building. Gently sloping, the fruit trees opened up into a carefully constructed open-air sanctuary. "This is our wilderness henge," Fred explained as we walked toward it. A little like a miniature Stonehenge, the sanctuary consisted of stones marking certain specific moments in the calendar. In fact, the sanctuary was essentially a reproduction of the cosmos, drawn exactly to scale and properly marked so that each step would have parallel meaning in terms of nature, cosmos, and the calendar.

It was getting somewhat cool now, and the thin robe wasn't enough to keep me from shivering, but the excitement of seeing an ancient Greek ritual reenacted precisely as it had been done in ancient Crete, a thousand years before Christ, dispelled all thoughts of catching a cold or being a little uncomfortable.

Since this was the festival of Samhain, better known as Hallowe'en, the appropriate incantations had to be made for that season of the year. The henge, from an old Anglo-Saxon term meaning "to hang," represents the entire cosmos. The boundary path around the henge stands for the horizon of the earth seen from the center, if one were to stand there and look out from it.

After invoking the goddess and the four quarters and in a sense dedicating ourselves to the spirit of nature communion expressed in this ceremony, we proceeded back to the house and assembled once again in the living room. Fred and Svetlana left us there for a while to prepare the temple itself, for the major part of the evening was yet to come.

For the next ten or fifteen minutes we chatted about the need to save what was left of nature in the Los Angeles area from expanding industry and pollution. Then Fred reappeared and beckoned us to follow him. The time was at hand for the mysteries to begin.

In ancient Greek witchcraft, or rather in the religious cult of Artemis, the Diana of the Celtic world, and Dionysos, the services are called mysteries—not in the sense of mystery stories of today, but relating to the term mysticism as we understand it at present.

Some things are veiled and are disclosed to the initiate at the proper time. Others must remain veiled forever. Entering the mysteries is a gradual and emotional experience. In so closely knit a group as Feraferia even the introductory step was not possible until the initiate had been properly prepared through studies and above all through the understanding of the ritual meaning inherent in Feraferia.

The word "Feraferia" is derived from Latin and means wildness festival. In writing of the principles of this group, which was founded in 1967, Fred Adams stated, "Wildness is the elusive quick of all spontaneous delicately urging life. The only way to reunite mankind is to reunite mankind with nature. Man will become humane toward man only when he becomes humane toward all nature. The inner nature of man has been disastrously severed from the all-enveloping nature of wilderness. The vital link between visionary nature within and ecological nature without is poetry."

As part of tonight's celebration, I was to be initiated so that I might then participate in the celebration called for by that particular season. One by one, we stepped into the adjoining room. It was very dark now as most of the lights had been doused. To the right was the door to the temple, a room so small that even half a dozen people would fill it. This was the inner sanctum of Kore, a room specially prepared by Fred and Svetlana, painted, adorned with sacred icons, altars in all four corners, a chair called "the chair of Demeter," and many ritual objects I am not permitted to describe here.

At the moment, however, that door was closed and I could see only very dim light coming from under it, the kind of light made by one or two candles. Some of the heavy incense being burned inside the temple escaped into the anteroom, and the sweet yet intoxicating smell of the strange aromatic made the entire proceedings even more remote to me. I had long forgotten where I was or that no more than two blocks away the Freeway traffic raced past. I was here to experience, firsthand, a very ancient ritual and to understand the pagan soul in such a way that through my eyes and heart, others might partake of it.

Silently, everyone took off his robe. Then the door to the

temple was opened and one by one we slowly stepped into the steaming inner temple. Priest and priestess took their places in the center, standing upon the sacred calendar engraved on the floor, while the others grouped themselves around in a circle. Stepping in last, I was motioned to stand opposite the priest inside the circle. The door was shut tight. A piece of cloth was immediately put over my head, preventing my seeing. Then the priest read the charge, or statement of intent, to me. Following this, there were some unearthly noises and it felt as if monsters were grappling my legs. However, I did not budge or show any fear. I expected this, of course, since I am quite familiar with the ancient mysteries.

After I had thus been symbolically tested, I was welcomed into the fold and permitted to kiss the sacred apple that represents the goddess.

In truth, though the entire initiation ceremony took no more than ten or fifteen minutes, I felt as if I had been away a year. As I stepped back into the adjoining room to return to the present, it seemed as if I were stepping down from Mount Olympus.

As a token of my initiation, I was handed a stone and wood sculpture, the work of Fred Adams, inscribed "Full moon over the mountain." The rest of the evening was social. Somehow Svetlana had managed to prepare cold cuts and wine and coffee, and with all tension gone, the evening was perhaps not so different from other evenings in Pasadena, California.

By midnight I was back in my Hollywood hotel room.

*

Since the ancient gods are merely various aspects of nature and since within us we have aspects of these gods, there may be many names by which one and the same deity is called. All pagan religions equate nature forces with various deities. In worshiping a seemingly independent deity existing somewhere outside oneself, one is in fact drawing upon one's inner forces, and in so doing, sparkplugs them into performing for oneself.

Kore, by the way, is "the magic maiden" or simply "the goddess." When the priestess greeted me with "welcome to the house of Ishtar," she was merely referring to another aspect of the Great Goddess. Just as "the magic maiden" inspires and causes beginnings, so the great "Mother Goddess," the later development of the same principle, attends to fulfillment of that which is promised.

Ishtar exists under one form or another in every religion. In the Old Testament, she is called Ashtorat. She was also known as Semiramis by the Assyrians, and to Greeks and Romans she was Aphrodite and Venus. To Celtic and Anglo-Saxon witches she is "the Queen of Heaven" or simply "the Mother Goddess." Even Christianity has taken some of her aspects in creating the image of the Madonna.

A female deity is very necessary for mankind to understand itself, because the female goddess stands at the beginning of life itself. Dr. Paul M. Vest, in an article called "Ishtar, Goddess of Love," says that "in the days of Ishtar, veneration of sexual phenomena was customary. It was mankind's primal response to the great force which is the direct source of all life. Consequently, adoration of sex and sex symbols was common to many early religions. And broadly speaking, the goddess Ishtar personified sex, fertility, and the female reproductive life force."

No orgies take place in Feraferia. No Psychedelic Venus Church here. The mechanics of sex are not stressed, but, rather, the spiritual unfoldment leading to love and being in tune with nature.

Fred Adams is a marvelously gifted painter. His interpretations of the mystery gods of ancient Greece rank favorably with some of the classical originals. At one point, he was interested in the American nudist movement but later discovered that the motivations of his mystic involvement differed greatly from the health aspects of nudism as it is generally known today. Whereas the shedding of clothes and playing in the sun seemed to be the main objectives of traditional nudism, Adams in Feraferia practices considers this only the first step in the right direction. Once the outer garments have been stripped off, it is necessary to attune the inner man to nature. Walking around a few hours without clothes and then returning to civilization and life as usual is not enough. Only when we readjust our thinking and feeling completely to total naturalness, whether we wear clothes or not, do we hold out hope that our civilization can still be saved from self-destruction.

That, in a nutshell, is the main point of Feraferia's philosophy. "The Feraferian vision includes new inspirations and new combinations from the most ancient wellsprings of the goddess. Innovations there are, but always in continuity with those ancient sources," Fred Adams explains. "You will find in the Feraferian vision no slavish archeological reconstructions, because the new paganism must accommodate all the new developments in human knowledge and awareness that have occurred since the old paganism quite deservedly lost its congregations and crumbled to ruin."

Adams calls the incantations for the days of the week "enchantments." The idea is not to beseech the goddess or to threaten her in order to force her to perform what is wanted, but rather to entice her, enchant her with charm, charisma, expressions of love and devotion. In other words, a positive approach to the goddess, all the way.

Mr. Adams is not only a great classical scholar with an amazing command of ancient Greek, but also quite a poet. The incantations here cited are mainly his work, even though they are based on ancient rituals and verbalizations and in essence express for modern man that which was similarly used by the ancient Greek worshiper in addressing *his* image of the goddess.

Beginning with Saturday, the day sacred to Saturn, the enchantments differ for each day of the week. These are not specific incantations but are rather like morning prayers in the Christian religion. In a way they are requests for guidance and the blessings of the day.

Ourania-Aphaia-Pheraia-Despoina, I dedicate this day to thee and to thine own land-sky-love-body of deep heaven, all stars, all grounds and matrices of existence, the geosphere, polar icecaps, tundra, and alpine fell.

Blessed be thy faerie realms. They will grow in wildness and love even as they suffuse my presence with joy and wilderness wisdom. Grant all wildlings in these realms thrive, find fulfillment and rebirth. I bestow my genius and love upon these realms and all their wildlings. May the wild realms of Ourania, black goddess of stars, bestow upon me their genius for mystery that divine ground essence, immanence transcendence, lasting value, eternity, wholeness, plurality, magistery, magnanimity, merging field cohesion, peace, cosmic completion, ultimate consummations. May I dance in the endless wedding procession of Ourania and Kronos, of alpine peaks and cone forests, as it winds through mazes of starlight in the nuptial night of the nameless bride! Evoe Kore! Evoe Kouros! Awiya!

After this prayer, whatever particular spells one wishes to make follow. Similar incantations and rituals have been created, or rather recreated, for each day of the week.

According to Mr. Adams, the proper time for cosmic communion is Saturday, the Sabbath and the night of Ourania, at 9:00 P.M. This is also the time for meditation and, of course, the meeting of covens. The second day of the week, Sunday, is sacred to Helios, the sun god. Monday is sacred to Artemis, and it is the third day of the week in the pagan calendar. Tuesday, the fourth day, belongs to Hermes-Pan, and Wednesday is sacred to Aphrodite. Thursday belongs to Ares, the god of war; Friday is dedicated to Kronos-Zeus-Godfather.

It is not my intention to publish here more than a few significant samples of Feraferia's and Fred Adams' poetic incantations. Let those who find in them inspiration gain the knowledge directly when they can immerse themselves in the study and practice of the cult itself.

Nevertheless, in addition to Saturday, the day of the Sabbath, perhaps the day of Diana, Monday, should also be singled out since many pagans who do not have access to Feraferia directly may want to know at least one valid ritual to use in some form of Dianic worship when the occasion arises.

Here, then, is the enchantment for Monday, the third day of the week:

Dione-Artemis-Selene-Hekate-Faerie-Diana-Aradia! I dedicate this day to thee and to thine own land-sky-love-body of waters: oceans, seas, lagoons, rivers, lakes, pools, springs, dew, mist, rain and snow; all cryptic communities of shade and soil; nocturnal air.

Blessed be thy faerie realms. They will grow in wildness and love even as they suffuse my presence with joy and wilderness wisdom. Grant all wildlings in these realms thrive, find fulfillment and continued rebirth. I bestow my genius and love upon these realms and all their wildlings. May the wild realms of Dione-Artemis, of Selene and Hekate, triune goddess of whirling dew-veiled night, bestow upon me their genius for: desire, imagination, vision, enchantment, inspiration, magic, fascination, delicacy, subtlety and wants, quality, influence, assimilation, empathy, fertility of soil, resistivity, sensitivity, creativity, poetry, music, Kore-care, charisma, tenderness, uniqueness, wonder.

May I forever hail and toast the divine wedding vows of the moon and the sun where they clasp each other—burning sands and frothing waters—along the far curving back of mighty earth. Evoe Kore! Evoe Kouros! Awiya!

This is again followed by the appropriate spells and incantations.

According to Mr. Adams the night of Diana is the proper time for such psychic enterprises as astral-projection, scrying, and magic. Nine P.M. is the proper hour for the circle of members of the coven to lie in star formation on the ground, heads together at the center, arms loosely touching all around. It is also a good time to trance-dance for specific magical purposes.

"The very backbone of the pagan movement is the calendar," Fred Adams explained. This does not mean the calendar in the conventional sense, but rather living completely in tune with the natural rhythm of life, doing whatever is appropriate at any given moment of the calendar and avoiding that which is contrary to its position.

Like all pagan movements, Feraferia celebrates a number of festivals during the calendar year. The beginning of the year, or vernal equinox, falls on March 21. It is called Ostara, and in the sacred circle it represents the East. Ostara celebrates the awakening in nature, the beginning of the new year, the end of winter. It is a joyous occasion and generally involves outdoor festivities.

Next comes Beltane, May Day, which is celebrated May 1. In Wicca, however, this holiday is marked on May eve, April 30. Beltane is described as "the festival of full flowering; sex crowns the holy nakedness of blossoming flesh. By sex the two are divided only to be molded closer in bliss."

Midsummer or the summer solstice is celebrated on June 21. This represents the longest day of the year and the full union in nature of all that is alive, "both in each," according to the Feraferia calendar.

August 1 is called Lammas or sometimes Lugnasad. This festival represents the height of summer fertility, the culmination of all that which man has strived for during winter and spring.

The autumnal equinox, on September 23, is a celebration of

homecoming. It represents the harvesting of the fruit, both in the field and in human experience.

November 1 is the day of Samhain, also called All Souls' Day and in Wicca celebrated the night before as Hallowe'en. Far from being a jolly occasion filled with levity, it is a thought-provoking day of reflection at the beginning of winter. In Wicca the reign of the horned god begins while the Mother Goddess rests. In Feraferia this is a time when new members may be initiated into the coven or when the "dread doors between worlds swing open." It is a time, then, for listening to the voices of the occult, both within and without.

On December 21, a day of thanksgiving is celebrated. It is also called a day of repose, since it signifies the return of the elements into the soil, when nature rests in preparation for the spring to come. The following day, December 22, is the day of Yule, or winter solstice. This is a celebration of first awakening, since at this point the sun turns north again, and heralds the coming of distant spring. Yule, therefore, is a joyous celebration, even though nature still sleeps.

February 10 is the festival of Olmelc, also known as Candlemas. This festival of the lights is called Brigid's Day in some Wicca covens because the prettiest member of the coven is selected to perform the ritual of Brigid, the eternal bride.

At the vernal equinox, March 21, the magic circle is completed and the new year begins.

*

Since 1967, Frederick Adams has published *Korythalia*, a newsletter of the new pagan movement. With it comes a monthly calendar called "Moon Mansions of the Magic Maiden." Here the twenty-eight days of the lunar month are given with their Greek names, the deities who rule them, and the elements in nature with which they connect. There are drawings of phases of the moon and poetic descriptions of what the moon seems to do to the eye of man. "Ishtar removing her veil" is the description for the new moon, while the full moon signifies "Ishtar removing her navel gem." The newsletter and calendar can be subscribed to for $4 a year from Post Office Box 691, Altadena, California 91001.

Recently Frederick Adams published what he calls the *Oracles of the Faerie Faith*. "The survival of human culture," Mr. Adams postulates, "depends on its psychic identification with ecologically viable styles of cultivation. This, in turn, depends on the creation of a new cultus of nature that stems from prehistoric sources while retaining everything of value that history has produced. Toward this new pagan synthesis of cult, culture, and cultivation in devotion to great nature Feraferia presents the following oracles."

The nine oracles to which Mr. Adams refers are *wildness*, that is to say, to live in nature and in tune with nature as it exists freely and not as it is planted or created; *faerie*, relating to arts and crafts as expressions of man's truly spontaneous genius of creation; *magic*, that which is possible beyond the causality as we know it, that is, poetry, and what Carl Jung has called "acausal synchronicity"; *divinity*, meaning a multitude of divine aspects rather than the solemn god-father image of monotheistic religions; *pantheism*, or the manifestations in nature represented by appropriate gods and goddesses corresponding to similar elements within each human being. To Feraferia these pantheistic deities include the Great Goddess, her two children Kore and Kouros, the seven gods and goddesses linking up with sun, moon, and the five visible planets, the tutelary spirits of specific nature regions, features, forms, and forces, and, finally, the faerie dance of ancestral spirits freely roving about while awaiting reincarnation—what in some occult philosophies are called elementals.

The sixth oracle of the faerie faith, according to Frederick Adams, is *paradise*, a sanctuary which the faith wishes to found where people can live the hesperian or paradisal way of life. These sanctuaries are the antithesis of city living, pollution, industrialization, centralization, and all that makes life miserable today.

How these sanctuaries will come into being and where they will be located, only the future can show. Some of the things representative of the hesperian way of life are organic gardening, concerned mainly with tree crops not grass crops; forestation; a diet of fruit and nuts, raw if possible; reverence for all animal life; freeing of all cattle and even pets; friendship with wild animals as free agents; harmlessness and pacifism; outside living in open-air dwellings made from natural materials, preferably in Southern climates; a maximum of work and play in the nude, using clothes only for protection and adornment, not for modesty; life in small villages with larger groups of people joining only for the celebration of special occasions. Adams has elaborated on this and many other concepts in a book called *The Hesperian Life—The Maiden Way*, first issued in 1957.

The seventh oracle of the faerie faith concerns *"the queen-dom of the trees."* Living by and among the great trees is an integral part of this faith, and for that reason reforestation and preservation of existing trees is of prime importance.

The eighth oracle is called *"community is freedom to love."* Since overpopulation would endanger the paradisal aspects of this visionary community, the fertility of the population would have to be curtailed. It is therefore necessary, Adams reasons, that libido be freed from reproductive applications and directed toward "nonrepressive sublimations of eros." The freedom to love, then, in this sense means fulfillment and enjoyment without fear of consequences.

Finally, the ninth oracle concerns itself with *"education for wildness and love."* Reeducating those coming from the cities and not yet in tune with the new pagan movement will be a prime requisite. "The arts of eros, especially rhapsodic dancing and singing, will prime each fiber of the body for all of love's delights and for the discharge of immense cosmic energies through magically informed erotic exchanges of every variety, so long as the heterosexual mode of the Divine Lovers predominates and no one is ever victimized." In a sense, this relates to the Wicca dictum, "An' it harm none, do what thou wilt."

In many ways Feraferia's theories are only a little ahead of current mores. In this day, when we speak of group sex and involvement and sensitivity training, that which was taboo not so long ago has become experimental, and what is experimental today may very well be the norm among some of tomorrow's advanced societies. Feraferia's prophet Frederick Adams states, "There is a decided connection between the antipagan waste of man's erotic potential and his laying waste of earth's ecological potential," meaning that frustrated people like to destroy what they cannot possess, while happy people prefer to see a happy world around them. "The fullest expression of kindness depends on the fullest experience of sensual grace. Love clusters of committed persons who constitute themselves experimental families will have the function of developing communal living and sexuality within the paradisal context."

As if to remind the reader of this manifesto that paradise has not yet been established on earth, and that the commonplace is still rampant all around us, there is a footnote at the bottom of this newsletter: "Feraferia so badly, badly, needs a volunteer typist, we will feed the lucky individual who dances forward celery hearts, ripe strawberries, and white wine from the lake of Niagara."

I ask you, who could resist such an invitation?

*

According to the calculations of the *Dictionary of Astrology* by Nicholas DeVore as interpreted by Feraferia, the last constellation visible before the sun rises on Ostara morning is Aquarius. This makes the Aquarian Age also the beginning of the new pagan era. The Aquarian Age, according to Frederick Adams and of course others, began with a rare celestial event on February 4, 1962. On that day, an eclipse occurred in Aquarius, during which all visible planets were in the same sign within twenty degrees of the exact conjunction of moon and sun.

The time is right, but author W. Holman Keith deplores the lack of great leadership among neopagans: "Sectarianism is the bane of the neopagan movement. There is freedom, which is all to the good, but unity is lacking." He points out that "no religious movement of thought and worship is more radical and significant for our time and the future than is neopaganism."

On a practical level, Feraferia believes that physical contact between the skin of man and the natural environment, that is to say, between flesh and plant, in activities they call "play-love-work" and which include sports, playfulness, and love-making, can actually work to the advantage of both. Man derives strength and revitalization from coming in contact with unspoiled wilderness, nature, growing things, plants and trees. Nature, on the other hand, by being touched directly by living bodies, obtains new energies with which to purify itself and to ensure its continued growth.

This conviction is, for instance, expressed in a ritual best undertaken at Beltane, or May Day, for the benefit of improving the landscape. "Some individuals or groups may enchant within actual grass environments at these times. If you make love *for* the grasses *in* the grasses, then you follow the most ancient and venerable precedence and newly initiate the most progressive psycho-religious processes of earth-self integration."

The ritual then continues, "The foreplay may be enjoyed as dance, ranging far and wide over the swards of Ares. As lovers caress each other on the move, clasp and unclasp while running and rolling through grass scapes, they at the same time caress, rub, pummel, and exchange blades and tufts of grass between them. Their beings become saturated with grassiness, until love longing is the very surge of chlorophyll. On the green wave of orgasm, they flow together into the landscape. Land and sky become their fused body of love, their unified land-sky-love-body."

This kind of activity, of course, requires not only privacy but a skin not yet so weakened by civilization that it is bothered by insect bites, pebbles, and sand and such, that prevents the participants from immersing themselves in a truly magnificent union with nature.

According to W. Holman Keith, the author who is frequently quoted as a kind of elder statesman by *Korythalia*, the principal difference between orthodox religions and the neopagan movement is the absence in orthodoxy of three divine principles: polytheism, or plurality of gods, perhaps better the multiple aspect of the deity, for even the pagan ultimately accepts that there is only one eternal divine force in the universe; fascination with its implied eroticism, which in paganism means erotic action, but with divine inspiration and eternal overtones; and exuberance, the wholly positive attitude toward life and all living creatures with its resulting rejection of violence, destruction, war, hunting and fishing, and any form of restriction contrary to natural law, be it spiritual or physical.

Keith rightly points out that the Bible speaks in amazement, "O Lord, how manifold are thy works!" The pagan simply uses different names for the various works of the Lord. He is well aware of the relationship between these various god principles, both toward each other and toward man, but in worshiping one principle, one symbolism, one deity at a time, man can put much more of himself into the ritual. He can visualize, sympathize with, even merge with that principle which he understands and which is responsible for the kind of action he requires or desires at any given moment. There isn't a shred less of divinity in pagan worship than there is in any orthodox religion. To the contrary, to the pagan all nature is holy. God is everywhere. God has many names.

To this Frederick Adams has added, "The primary sacrament

and paradigm of cosmic process is the wild play and sweet union of the sexes, which eternizes both the unique and the universal infusion of giving and taking and in the supreme communion, Both in Each. The great divide of gender is the root condition of all being and becoming, and of the uncompromised approximation of the coming to being."

*

One need only take one good look at the Los Angeles countryside to realize that the building of paradise will require major efforts, either in physical distance or in the removal of existing clutter. But the followers of nature religions need not wait for this somewhat distant moment to enjoy at least some meaningful communion with nature. Many people in Southern California have gardens in back of their houses. Just as the Englishman feels that his home is his castle, so the Feraferian considers his garden his sacred precinct where he can do as he pleases. So far, no intrusion of privacy has occurred where people have worshiped whatever deities they choose to call their own within their houses or gardens. I doubt that even a neighbor's interference could stand up in a court of law unless something along the lines of a public nuisance could be proven. The gentle Feraferians are not only no public nuisances, they are not even private nuisances. Although they are perfectly entitled to conduct those rituals requiring nudity in their gardens, they have not done so in order to avoid any form of controversy.

*

Fred Adams' wilderhenge need not be the only one, however. Anyone wishing to worship Kore, the magic maiden, can do so in a henge of his own construction. The spot chosen should be appealing for reasons of beauty and have a certain sense of what Fred Adams calls "aliveness."

First one must drive a stake into the center of the chosen area and mark off a circle of at least ten feet in diameter. The circle may be larger, if that is possible. Around this circle one must dig a shallow ditch about eight inches wide and deep, which represents the round river of the sacred year. This is the preliminary step. On the first clear, moonless night one must go out into the garden or back yard and drive a stake into the soil near the inside edge of the shallow ditch representing the round river. The spot is a point where a line drawn from the center of the circle crosses the ditch and thereby seems to connect to Polaris, better known as the North Star.

The following day, a line must be drawn from the Yule point, which is the spot one has marked the previous night, through the center, and onto the midsummer point, or south on the opposite side. There another stake is to be driven into the ground. In similar manner, the east and west points are marked off, with either chains or ropes or tapes, and stakes driven into the soil at the east and west points. Then the four points midway between the cardinal points are marked off in such a way that all eight points by the edge of the round river are an equal distance from each other. Stone or wooden markers called menhirs are then placed on these eight spots and the center.

*

As far as the spheres of the gods are concerned, Adams explains that these are astral realms surrounding the planets, the sun, and the moon. By a magical extension of the relativity theory, psychic and divine aspects are added to the gravitational field surrounding every heavenly body.

"When pagans prepare their henge or faerie ring for the avocation of wild realms," Fred Adams explains, "by the magic of imagination they witness these planetary spheres converging within the circle, since it is a condensation of earth-in-cosmos."

He refers to these magic operations as eco-psychic, meaning that the spirit of wilderness represented by Kore, from which comes all life, is contained in the totality of the landscape not just in the minds of men, but also in the environment.

"There is a way of laying the planetary spheres on the henge to form a psycho-cosmic tuning dial, equivalent to the sefirah tree of Kabbalah, but more appropriate to newly emerging pagan consciousness." In a sense, the magic henge works on a prin- ciple similar to a listening device aimed into outer space to catch the faint signals from distant stars and enlarge them so they can be understood on earth. This system draws upon the emanations from planets and stars and from nature on this planet and pulls these forces into the small area of the henge. The result, of course, is that by being compressed into a relatively small area, these powers become condensed and tre- mendously effective. When these forces are then enlarged by the human powers within the bodies and minds of the partici- pants in celebrations, we have a considerable reservoir of energy requiring only channeling and direction to become a realistic force capable of accomplishing specific tasks.

The moon is the most powerful influence in the heavens, being closer to us than any other celestial body. Thus, the utilization of the moon's radiation in certain rituals, forms an important part of Feraferia's activities.

The moon has thirty phases, one half of which are waxing, or increasing in size as we see her here on earth, and the other half waning, or decreasing her apparent size. When the moon is waxing, that is to say, during phases one through fourteen, she is sending us cosmic energies, and it is a good time to start projects requiring energy. It is also the best time for rituals. In the thinking of Feraferia, a ritual is an active externalization magic. During the waning phase of the moon, inward activities, such as meditation, are better. Between phases one and eight, until the turn of the moon is reached, cere- monials calling for gaiety, fancy, whimsicality are called for. From phases eight through fourteen, as the moon increases in apparent size, the stimulation of appetite, the deepening of passion, and the maturation of ourselves are best emphasized.

At the time of the full moon, phases fourteen to sixteen,

the time of the Sabbath is at hand. At such times, the moon assists, as Adams puts it, "the most vivid and festive exhilarations of love, and the fulfillment of psychosomatic interactions." Contrary to popularly held views concerning the waning moon, that period is not unsuitable for occult practices but merely holds different values. "When the moon is waning," Adams explains, "the mystic intimacy between interstellar distances is waxing. As the white moon diminishes, the black moon unfolds."

The waning power of the moon apparently draws energies out of the earth and sends them toward heaven, thus reversing the flow. During the waning phases, the operator of magic practices would best contact his or her own inner depths, the unconscious, the occult.

Assuming that one has created one's own henge to worship in the pagan manner and is ready to use it, there is still the matter of a proper incantation. How does one approach the sacred precinct for the first time? Through its poetic high priest, Feraferia suggests the following prayer:

> We stand before the temple of Great Nature, mandala of the sacred year, mandala of the sacred self, psycho-cosmic tuning dial of an eternal metamorphosis through perennial sacrament. Hail, Great Goddess. Evoe Kore! Harken to the mythologos of the sacred year. We worship the divine lovers, eternal goddess of nature and containment and perennial god of purpose and penetration. Their union is the pattern of creation. They are the protogenesis of all things. Their celestrial thrones are moon and sun. Their love round of the year is the everlasting religion of nature, the inspired dance of the seasons. Evoe Kore. Evoe Kouros. Awiya!

The purpose of worshiping in the henge is to commune with the reality of whatever divinity or deity is being addressed. "If we open ourselves sufficiently to the landscapes of earth, the divinities residing therein will identify themselves in their characteristic resonances, their sensory and intuitional complexes." The deities worshiped in this manner do exist in reality and are not just symbols, in the view of Feraferia, although one may regard them symbolically as well. But the more one can accept these deities as being real personalities, the stronger will be the relationship between worshiper and deity. The rituals have overtones of the dramatic, the theatrical, because in the view of this cult, the arts and crafts are "handmaidens of religion."

*

In the summer of 1970, various pagan groups active in the Los Angeles area met for an informal discussion of principles to see whether they could work together under an overall organization. That organization became the Council of Themis and it is still in existence. From the discussions, followed by "small-scale feasting," there emerged eight statements of principle, to which all participating groups could subscribe.

These pagans felt that the two principal "articles of faith" concerned the nature of their deity. The first statement, therefore, concerns polytheism: "Polytheism begins with the female and male principles, the goddess and god, divine lovers, from whose love all creation is derived. The multiplicity of goddess and god individualities are aspects of the infinite variety of creation, stemming from goddess and god. Slightly revising a saying, it may be asserted that the omnipotence of divinity is merely another word for its polytheist unity."

The second most important "article of faith" agreed upon at the conference concerns the principle divinity focus of worship: "Worship focuses on goddess and god as divine lovers, bride and groom, eternal feminine source and perennial masculine quickening, protogenesis of all things: worlds, gods, nature, men, and so forth."

Next came freedom of worship: "Worship, as an essential part of religious practice, is both a venerating of and a communing with divinity. Because people are unique individuals, they differ in their images, conceptions, and experiences of divinity and in their ways of worshiping as well. Therefore, freedom of worship is an indispensable condition of their development and fulfillment as human beings, so long as their worship imposes no undue hardship on others."

Of increasing importance is the next "article of faith" agreed upon by the six participating groups in the Los Angeles area. It concerns the worship of nature and our attitude toward ecology: "Nature is divinity made manifest, the perennial love feast of the divine lovers, goddess and god . . . creativity, continuity, balance, beauty, and truth of life. Of all man's secular studies, ecology comes perhaps closest to bringing him to the threshold of a reverent attitude toward his world and its inhabitants. Ecology not only confirms the wonders of form and function that other secular studies have revealed, but it brings these into organic union with each other as one dynamic, living whole; and it indicates the conditions for the well-being of both this overall unity and the parts that compose it. An intensive realization of these conditions, and of one's own immediate role in their sustainment and development, brings one to the threshold of religious experience. To worship nature, therefore, is to venerate and commune with divinity as the dynamically organic perfection of the whole."

The fifth "article of faith" concerns an area of human expression easily misunderstood or misinterpreted, or, if taken out of context and unduly emphasized, likely to cast a distorted image of paganism as a whole. Eroticism is derived from Eros, a god of love: "Love is the essence of divinity, and is the creative action of the universe. Eroticism in its religious reference, venerates love play in the sexual act as divine, as creative physical expression of our union with nature as we reconcile and unite sexual opposites. Hence, love play and sex are natural and beautiful whenever shared in mutual consent. Sexual freedom in this comprehensive sense is a primary doctrine of many pagan religions. It is the freedom to express love, sensually, to be physically natural, to be at one with nature in the effectual functioning of the physical being, and to be free from guilt due to repressive, antinatural conditioning. To deny or denigrate sexuality in man is to deny or denigrate nature and divinity."

Next comes the subject of violence and aggression: "We try to create in practice a style of living in which violence and the occasion for it are progressively reduced through both our own inner growth and our way of dealing with the outer affairs and conditions of our lives. We deplore and censure all wanton violence and destruction, all murder, all habitual coercion, including habitually punitive attitudes and practices. Defense of home and loved ones against immediate threat of death or severe suffering is a natural reflex. When finesse fails to deflect or thwart such aggression, coercion and/or violence would seem to be the only recourse."

The seventh "article of faith" dealt with the subject of reincarnation or what pagans call "life between death and rebirth": "A vigorous and wholehearted living in *this* life, in *this* time-and-space world, does negate the idea that this life in this world should be submitted as a matter of policy to restraint and chastisement, especially in its sensuous aspects for the supposed benefits of a future, after-death life or condition. Belief is asserted in reincarnation as a periodic flowering of the soul in sensuous flesh, in an objective body among objective surroundings. The quality and direction of our activities is by no means without definite implications for the conditions of a soul's life between bodily death and rebirth."

Finally, the eighth "article of faith" the six pagan groups agreed upon as mutually binding and acceptable to them concerns the sacred myths: "The sacred myths are a tapestry of truths, but are not to be interpreted as reports of historical events. They are a dimension of theological reality, a wondrous and inspired form of religious art."

The myths referred to here are the stories of mythological

gods, goddesses and heroes ranging from the ancient Greek
and Egyptian pantheons through the Celtic and American Indian mythological canvases into Far Eastern concepts of divinity—in short, all of mankind's mythological distillations and
exteriorizations. For it can be seen that there is much duplication
and there are many parallels among the mythological concepts
of different nationalities, even though these nations may not
have had any actual contact with each other. Thus it appears
that all this material may very well derive from a common
source, a source not as yet fully understood and perhaps forever
beyond human reach. What we can grasp, however, are the
implications as they concern us, the living, on this planet earth.

*

When it appeared that I might spend late October of 1970
in the Los Angeles area, I asked Fred whether I might take
part in their Hallowe'en ritual. A note from Svetlana informed
me that the night of October 30 they would perform a "whole
earth invocation." Since this would be performed at night it
would in effect be the beginning of Hallowe'en whereas Wicca
rituals are generally done the night of Hallowe'en itself.

There were nine of us present. The ritual of invoking the
various aspects of Mother Earth was performed mainly outdoors. Everyone wore black robes and, except for me, had his
face covered by hoods. My robe, unfortunately, did not have a
hood but no one seemed to mind.

In a ritually carefully planned manner the priest and priestess
followed by the other participants opened the "astral doors"
of the henge. Entering the henge between northeast and east,
"they slide giddily down the other side into the Faerie Ring
Between Worlds." When each celebrant was at his or her
proper station, the spirits of the four quarters were invoked,
followed by the spirits of the hours and seasons. After they
invoked the elemental spirits, the enchanters had "recreated
the universe in eco-psychic terms, that is, in terms of a spiritual
relativity respecting man-in-earth."

The priestess was then seated in the center of the ring representing "the nameless bride." At this point the actual ceremonial undertaking began. Carrying a wand, the priestess moved from menhir or subdivision to subdivision speaking the sacred incantations and performing certain ritual dance steps. Finally she returned to the point of departure. This signified that all the Mighty Ones of earth and sky were present around the altar dedicated to Kore and that the further celebration could commence. The entire proceedings took about twenty minutes.

At this point, the priestess followed by the priest and the rest of the congregation made her way back into the house to continue their worship indoors. After a short pause, which gave Fred a chance to prepare the inner temple for the secret ritual that was to follow, the group entered the tiny temple itself. It was very difficult for all of us to get inside, but somehow we managed, standing in a tight circle around the center in which the ritual was being performed by priest and priestess.

We still wore our black robes, but the priestly couple had changed to different robes in keeping with the nature of the occasion. With the help of tarot cards, the priest then evoked, step by step, the various qualities of the goddess, equating forces of nature with parts of her physical body. From time to time, the group would dance around the center as best it could invoking the goddess and stopping abruptly to let the energy thus generated permeate the temple.

With the ceremonial kiss of the sacred apple that represented the goddess, the ritual ended.

*

I saw Fred Adams again on Candlemas, February 6, 1971. A friend had expressed a desire to be initiated into the preliminary grade. Wearing black robes and cords, we performed the "midwinter" ceremony in keeping with the season. I had given Fred a small terracotta statuette of the goddess Astarte that dated from second-century Egypt. The figure was officially welcomed into the fold and placed ceremoniously upon the western altar of the outer sanctuary.

One of the reasons why some of my experiences and some of the material used in the initiations cannot be published here and must remain reserved for those who become initiates themselves at the proper time is the need for the element of surprise. "It is certainly one of the most effective aspects of any initiation that really 'takes,'" Fred Adams explained somewhat apologetically, "and it helps the mystes or initiate to continue to initiate himself after the formal 'jolt,' much in the same way education becomes a lifelong process of self-actualization after the 'instruments' of this process are obtained from formal curricula."

It was time now for a dedication ceremony indoors honoring Candlemas. Consequently, lights were very prominent, and both priest and priestess carried lighted candles around the sacred circle laid out on the floor of the outer temple. As they moved about ceremoniously, they chanted the poetic reinterpretation of the ancient liturgical invocations, sometimes alternating, sometimes in unison:

"I am the infant sun of Ostara or lady day on the eastern end of the equinox aligned. O full moon, queen of unfurling buds, enchant the Ostara menhir of the East, dawn and spring."

Svetlana continued the incantation alone.

"Onnn," she intoned, and then she continued the incantation: "Here begins the arc of vernal alliance as I am the herald of winds that swirl in my lungs like drafty jets causing the chasm of mountain ranges. . . ."

This was followed by "Evoe ecos," and to the accompaniment of a tambourine she took some ritual dance steps around the circle.

Next, it was Fred who continued: "The new moon is reborn. Evoe kallistos Artemis." About half of the rituals at Feraferia are in the ancient Greek language, which Fred Adams understands perfectly. Artemis, of course, is Diana, goddess of the moon, identified here with the magic maiden and Kore.

"I am the ithyphallic adolescent sun of Beltane, or May Day," Fred went on. "O full moon, queen of voluptuous boons, enchant the Beltane menhir of the Southeast of midmorning and spring season at high tide."

This was followed by the invocation of the other positions of the sun until the original position had once again been reached. Together with the incantations, they performed the ritual steps, taking great care that the candles did not set fire to the house. Quite obviously, this ritual was much easier to do outside, but it was an exceptionally cold night and the neighbors had been curious of late, so Fred had decided to try to do it indoors for a change.

Finally, priest and priestess had gone through the entire invocation and returned to their original positions.

For a few minutes we sat around and chatted, for the impressive ceremony we had just witnessed gave us food for thought. My friend Patricia, for whom all this was entirely new even though she had studied witchcraft and the neopagan religions assiduously prior to being invited, seemed misty-eyed with excitement and the novelty of it all. She is by profession a medical X-ray technician and by avocation a student at the Police Academy, for she wants to become a deputy sheriff. This world was about as far removed from her ordinary surroundings as anything could be.

A little while later the inner temple was ready to receive us and Patricia would now be introduced to the preliminary grade, a kind of novice's rank, in Feraferia. Again, wearing black robes, we entered the inner temple. The new member-to-be was stationed on the perimeter of the calendar design engraved on the floor. I stood across from her on the other side of the calendar.

While Fred invoked various elements as they related to parts of the body, Svetlana coaxed the goddess to descend: "Kore, spirit, now appear in mystery raiment of the year." This was followed by the metallic sound of the sistrum, a musical instrument of Egyptian origin. Striking the sistrum, the priestess then danced around the center as part of the enchantment directed toward the spirit of Kore.

After each round of enchantment, the priest continued the incantation, gradually going through the months of the calendar one by one and correlating them with various parts of the human body. The names of the months are the old Celtic designations, just as the entire Feraferia cult is a strange intermixture of Greek, Celtic, and even American Indian elements. "Month of Quirt, apple month in the biome body of the holy maiden. All broad leaf evergreen forests become our skin and love zones," Fred intoned, "the erogenous zones of the body by skin and erogenous zones of thy perfect body, by grace of magic maiden is conferred upon thee from broad leaf evergreen forests."

A total of twenty-two such descriptive incantations were read by the priest to the new member while, with the twenty-second pronouncement, her "perfect resurrection body" had been conferred on Patricia. All she had to do was just stand there and listen, while the priest and priestess together intoned the closing verses: "O holy maiden of the kindling quick, surging mist and mazing echo, the innocent bounty of the trees bears thy faerie flesh of wildness, wonder, magic, mirth and love. . . ."

Slowly we walked out of the temple back to the living room. After a period of rest Fred summoned me back alone. This time Patricia, the new novice, had to stay behind. Despite the lateness of the hour, I was to be raised to a higher degree of initiation. Seated in the "chair of Demeter," I quietly listened as the priest with the help of the priestess performed the magic ceremony. Then I was given a piece of black cloth in the shape of a veil as a token of the occasion.

I am not at liberty to disclose what was said, but I felt strange and stranger yet after I had left the sacred precincts of the House of Ishtar. It was as if some chord had been struck, a chord that continued to reverberate inside me and imbue me with a greater understanding of nature, both within and without. I haven't been quite the same since. To be sure, my logical thinking, my power of reasoning, and my worldly affairs have in no way been affected. If anything, I am sharper than I was six months ago, but my emotional self seems to have undergone some strange developments. Somehow I am able to feel differently, accept fate more understandingly, and give to others more of myself than I was ever able to before.

*

It may be years before cults like Feraferia become mass movements, if they ever do. But even sporadic groups working throughout the country and the world might sufficiently change the course of destruction on which most of humanity is now traveling, or at least slow down the end results.

I found my initiation into the mysteries of Feraferia a rewarding and unique experience. It does not conflict with anything else I hold dear, nor with any religion I might practice, whether Christian or pagan. It merely makes them all more meaningful.

Feraferia is not for everyone, nor should everyone think that Feraferia is for him, or that he will be accepted for membership. All ancient mysteries were selective in their admission of new members. This must be so to preserve the power, the integrity, the purpose of the cult. Thinning the blood makes it weaker; spreading the secret truths too far afield lessens their impact where they are most needed.

*

I mentioned Sára Cunningham when I discussed the heirs of Wicca. When I first met Sára a few years ago she was living in the Hollywood hills in a delightful semidilapidated house that even the most experienced taxi drivers had difficulty locating. The house was filled to the brim with the paraphernalia of witchcraft, ranging from herbs, dried ritual objects, even animals, to books and the tools of her witchcraft trade. For Sára was then, and is now, a teacher in the ancient art of witchcraft. Her pupils range from students eager to learn the occult through the backdoor, so to speak, rather than at U.C.L.A., to such motion-picture luminaries as Susan Cabot and June Lockhart. These people weren't necessarily practicing witches, but they came to listen to Sára as friends and because they were interested in the many aspects of the occult in which Sára Cunningham is an expert.

In the summer of 1970, Sára decided to turn her priestly activities in another direction. Long a student of Egyptian religion and well aware of the Egyptian origins of much of Celtic Wicca, she felt that the Egyptian ritual was more suited to her emotionally at that time in her life. Consequently, she established a temple dedicated to the main Egyptian gods, Iris, Osiris, and Ra. When she heard that I was coming again to Pasadena, she not only invited me to her new temple, but offered to let me film a portion of one of her rituals for my documentary on pagan religions.

The Church of the Eternal Source, as she has called her temple, is the refounded church of ancient Egypt in which the original gods of mankind are worshiped by their original names. "Communications with the gods is practiced through intuitive sciences such as ritual worship, astrology, personal meditation, Yoga, and divination, including the tarot and I Ching," Sára explained.

Thus, the worshiper may get to understand the will of the gods and as a result expand consciousness and evolve spiritually. This, Sára feels, will put one in harmony with divine forces and of course with one's own self. Since ancient Egypt enjoyed a long period of prosperity and peace under these same gods, it is hoped that worshiping them will produce similar conditions in our society.

The problem of polytheistic worship, of having more than

one god to pray to, does not faze the Church of the Eternal Source. The high priestess points out that Christianity also worships four distinct deities, the Holy Father, the Holy Mother, the Son, and the Holy Spirit. What she calls the "multiplicity of the godhead" is reached through study and concentration by her students and this in turn leads them to an understanding and acceptance of human diversity.

Everyone seems to be welcome in this group. "As the gods appear to each person solely in respect to his accomplishments in this and past lives, no discrimination on account of ancestry or previous religious or political affiliation is practiced," Sára explains. Psychic and spiritually evolved individuals are particularly welcome in the group. The church is supported by free-will donations, is incorporated in California as a religious institution, and offers a complete educational program "leading ultimately to the doctor of divinity degree and priestly orders." There is a "pyramid of initiation" comprising nine different steps from the lowest, called aspirant, followed by brother or sister, neophyte, zelator, in turn followed by the novitiate, then the proselyte, finally the initiate, priest, and high priest. Distinctive colors, dress, and astrological concepts are attached to each step. Since the church conducts public prayer services, there is nothing secretive about it, at least not in the initial stages.

Unquestionably, the higher degrees are conferred only after serious study and other conditions. Publication of ritual and pledges in this book was not allowed. But the Church of the Eternal Source publishes a kind of newsletter (Post Office Box 2942 in Pasadena, California), and anyone wishing to be an ancient Egyptian rather than a modern Christian has a chance to do so under the sunny skies of Southern California. True, there are no pyramids around and the buildings on main street are far from majestic, but you can forget all that once you are inside Sára's temple.

The temple is located in the upstairs part of a rambling

old wooden structure she calls home. It is probably one of
the oldest buildings in Pasadena, surrounded by trees and set
within a small garden. From the veranda one enters the living
room, a comfortable and mystically decorated place. To the
left is a room she uses for her classes and lectures. Up the stairs
there are two rooms to each side of the landing. To the right
is Sára's private study and inner temple where she continues
to worship in the Wicca tradition. Acquiring Egyptian ritual
in no way forces one to dispose of earlier religious convictions
and Sára still rightfully considers herself a high priestess of
the Wicca.

To the left of the staircase is her Egyptian temple. Since her
priests are all professional artists and she herself is a very fine
painter and sculptress, the room is truly magnificent within
the context of its size and proportions.

Painstakingly, these people have reproduced the Egyptian
designs required for such a place. The altar was handmade
from specifications derived from ancient sources. Large, life-size
paintings of the gods of ancient Egypt adorn the walls. Even
the tools of the Egyptian priesthood have been made by the
group themselves including a pipe, sistrum, a bell, and, of course,
a large ankh—a large T-shaped cross surmounted by a loop and
symbolizing life.

While I was waiting for the temple to be prepared for the
ceremony to follow, I admired some of the necklaces Sára makes.
Some of these are fertility symbols such as the Blue Goddess,
while others are representations of the zodiac. They are strung
onto bead necklaces and made up by Sára in small quantities
to be sold at very little profit to her friends and those who want
to wear a sacred witchcraft necklace.

As a token of good luck for the incipient temple, I had
brought along a genuine Egyptian relic dating back to pre-
Christian times. The small terracotta ushabti was to be received and installed ceremoniously in another few moments.

(An ushabti is the figure of a worker who will do the deceased's work in the world beyond.)

Shortly after, Sára reappeared in heavy Egyptian makeup and wearing her robe of office adorned with jewelry closely copied from Egyptian models that prevailed at the height of Egypt's civilization. Her three male companions, the priests of Osiris, Ra, and Toth, were splendidly attired in white robes. Since I am a professional archeologist and familiar with the traditional outfits worn by worshipers for such occasions, I had brought a white robe myself, though it was simple and in no way comparable to the artistic robes worn by my hosts.

Leaving behind some friends and students who happened to be there that evening, we ascended the stairs, and entered the temple, which was heavily scented with incense. The door was shut and the six of us, two women and four men were ready for the ceremony to welcome the little relic into its new home.

"Omen, omen, omen, omen," the group intoned, breathing in deeply and singing out the sound that was to establish the proper vibrations for the occasion. At the same time, the sistrum was rattled. This was followed by an incantation in ancient Egyptian. Then Sára, in a voice filled with deep emotion, raised her hands to the sky and called out, "Adoration unto thee, O lotus queen of heaven, blessed mother. Hail unto thee, O mighty Isis! May this ritual find favor in thine eyes. Grant thy blessings unto thy children. Be with us this night. Omen, omen."

This was followed by some rattling of the sistrum and further intonation of Egyptian sentences. Then the priest of Amun-Ra approached the altar as Sára stepped to one side. It was now his turn to invoke his particular tutelary deity, and this he did in a mixture of ancient Egyptian and ritual English. Having hailed Ra and asked his presence in our midst, he continued, "Thou art the first and last light; thine eyes are the sun and the moon; we call thee by thy ancient name

Hara; thou art Apollo; thou art Mercury; thou art Mars; thou art Christos; thou art light; thou art music; thou art lust; thou art freedom; those who serve, let us serve thee. Divine initiator, help us achieve our aspirations. We call thee by thy true name, Hara."

*

In most religions, especially the mystery religions, it was considered wrong to call the gods by their proper names. Instead, synonyms or descriptive words were used. "Thou shalt not take the name of thy Lord in vain," the Bible teaches us, and in the orthodox Hebrew religion the name Yahweh or Jehovah is never used. Instead, the term Adonai must be pronounced even though the letters spell Yahweh or Jehovah. This is a very ancient concept. The idea is that one must reserve the actual name of the god for very secret and very important occasions; otherwise his power will be lessened.

It is from that point of view that the Egyptian worshipers at Pasadena pointed out that they were calling to their god by his proper name, thus showing that their mission was an important one and they expected him to come forth and be recognized.

*

Now the priest of Osiris stepped up to the altar and invoked his god. "Homage to thee, Osiris, lord of eternity, king of gods, whose names are manifold, whose forms are holy. Thou art the beneficial spirit amongst spirits, god of celestial oceans. Drop from thee its waters. Assa, assa, Ra, thou art one. Rebirth." Now the others chimed in with the ritual intonation of "omen, omen, omen!"

After the two others had also stepped up and invoked their respective deities, the little idol was presented to Isis, put into a ceremonial container and properly accepted and blessed. Then the high priestess closed the circle, and one by one we filed out of the temple. In the other room upstairs we changed back into civilian clothes.

Maybe I didn't feel the presence of ancient Egypt's gods within me the way these worshipers may very well feel them since they come here so often and have risen spiritually over a long period of time, but I did feel an almost total alienation from the physical world outside, as if I were indeed enveloped by something other than the already polluted California air. The vibrations at Sára Cunningham's Egyptian temple are genuine whether her magic is Egyptian or Wicca. Perhaps it seems somewhat incongruous for people in the 1970's to go back to ancient Egypt for their religious experience. One might argue that being bizarre compensates for the disappointments and routine assignments of everyday life. Dressing up for the part, the dramatic show-business-like ritual, the strange environment of the temple, would of course create in student or worshiper the feeling of being different from the rest of the community. Since all pagan religions teach that the gods are within oneself as well as on the outside, this would only indicate another form of searching for one's own identity. The absence of the Christian doctrine of original sin and of identification with the suffering of Jesus makes it a joyous religion, creating in turn a more positive personality.

That at least seemed to me the result of taking part in these rituals.

*

"Thou art god!" says the *Green Egg*, mimeographed newsletter of the Church of All Worlds (Post Office Box 2953, St. Louis, Missouri). This is a catchall of neopagan thought, American Indian thinking, witchcraft, ecology, and the sort of thing that goes down well with an increasing number of young people. It isn't particularly friendly to the Establishment nor is it particularly politically radical. A large portion of the newsletter is devoted to the reprinting of letters to the editor and to the exchange of ideas in letter form. A lot of it is personal. None of it is sexually extreme the way the Psychedelic Church of San Francisco might put it. But it is part of the young movement toward pantheistic faith.

When the *Green Egg* says, "Thou art god," it fails to add, "and god is in thee." That, however, is the essence of all pagan thought.

I found a far gentler religion with very little interest in the political scene per se in a Mediterranean-oriented pagan cult called Sabaeanism. The master mind of this movement is a dark-haired, slim young man of aristocratic bearing named Frederic de Arechaga. In either his late twenties or his very early thirties, he dresses in the most elegant Spanish styles, which is not surprising since he is of Spanish origin. Mr. de Arechaga speaks perfect English, choosing his words with great care and literacy. He makes a living with an occult shop called "El-Sabarum" on North Halstead Street in Chicago. There you can buy occult supplies of every kind from candles to jewelry and robes whether you are a member of his Sabaean Society or not. There, too, you can pick up a copy of the society's newsletter called *Janus*, which contains a lunar calendar and fairly sophisticated discussions of witchcraft and of the meanings of gods and goddesses.

In many ways the Sabaeans follow the astrological ecological principles expounded to me by Fred Adams and his Feraferia group in Pasadena, but there are important differences. Above all, Feraferia's traditions are mainly ancient Greek intermingled with some Celtic ritual. The Sabaeans are a Mediterranean cult that has remained alive through centuries of persecution in the general area of Spain and Portugal. I had never heard of Mr. de Arechaga and his Sabaeans until he and the cult were brought to my attention by my Chicago friend Carole Burton. Although an initiate of the Wicca, Carole had been to some of the Sabaean Society gatherings and had studied under de Arechaga.

We talked briefly on the telephone and then de Arechaga offered to meet me in my suite at the Oxford House. Over lunch we discussed his particular brand of paganism and what its aims were in today's changing world.

It appears that the term *saba* comes from the Holy Koran. "We have a special philosophy," de Arechaga explained. "We relate to the Old Religion, but we do not believe in hero worship. We eliminate competition and the need to identify. Consequently, we do not like to speak of ourselves, but rather of ideas." De Arechaga inherited his paganism from his mother. She had been a high priestess in Spain, and pagan traditions go back a long time in his family. In calling his philosophy Sabaean, he refers to a very ancient tradition antedating both Christianity and Mohammedanism. This was the religion of Spain in the Megalithic Age.

"What are the basic tenets of your philosophy?" I asked.

De Arechaga smiled and shook his head. "It is very difficult to put into a few words. We have the Mother Goddess and believe in matriarchy. We do not have any dogma. When we come to the question as to why we are alive we like to quote a riddle: 'The purpose of life lies in what is it that you are born without that when you die is the only thing you take with you?'"

I looked at him, somewhat puzzled. He explained, "It is that which nobody else will ever know because during your lifetime you may have a chance to find out. It is what you learn, your wisdom. We are identified with the great Mother Goddess. I am all that is, was, and ever shall be. Our god is a divinity with two faces, which relates to the sixty-fourth chapter of the Egyptian Book of the Dead. Because we are yesterday, today, and tomorrow, what purpose would there be in knowing tomorrow if you could not change it today? There is only one reality we believe in, and that is the reality of *now*. Reality is your personal experience. We are not hedonistic. We are henotheistic."

Again I must have appeared very puzzled to the young man. "Henotheistic," he explained, "means that we are the only philos-

ophy in the world that can actually admit an atheist in our
midst, because henotheism is the sum metamorphosis of mono-
theism, polytheism, pantheism, and so on. The reason we can
accept atheism is because the relationship between man and
divinity lies in himself. We say you *are* god; therefore god does
not need you since you are it."

I realized that here again was a fundamental difference between the paganism of de Arechaga and that of Fred Adams.

The gentleman from Spain explained further, "This hand
is me, but I am not this hand so I am god, but god is not I.
That's where presumption comes in, and righteousness prevails
in the individual thinking that god is him as well."

"Do you accept any deities actually existing outside our
world?" I asked.

De Arechaga nodded emphatically, "Many! Divinity, as we
view it, is saba, which means all. This word has meaning in
Arabic and Egyptian. The Jews have a similar word, *tzaba*,
and *sheba* also means all. It means the worship "of the host
of heaven." We have the key in the ritual. The purpose of
ritual as we understand it is to relate with that around you
which includes the heavens. When an individual is interested in
the occult and does not understand astronomy, he will fail. We
believe that an astrologer should be an astronomer first."

"Then astrology plays a part in your ritual?" I interjected.

"Very much so. Astrology to us is vital."

I wanted to bring the discussion down to actual ritual, to the
fundamental experience of the cult itself as it appeared to those
taking part in it.

"Do you have holidays on which certain rites are performed?"
I asked.

"The greater and lesser Sabbaths. We relate to the heaven
and the gods who relate to the planets and so forth. The
identity with the moon and the sun is extremely predominant.
The identity with the moon causes the Sabbath, or *shabbati*,
which is a Sumerian term, by the way, not Jewish. *Shabbati*

is a period of the moon; it divides into one, which is a month, into two, into four, into seven. Seven periods of the moon are the days of the week, and thus each day of the week relates to each god."

"What does your Sabbath ritual consist of?"

"The whole purpose of ritual, as far as we're concerned, is for personal gain. No matter how philanthropic you want to appear, you're still doing it for personal satisfaction."

"Personal gain in which areas?"

"It could be anything from money and love to simply the self-satisfaction that you have done it. You know, the idea of power."

"And this is derived from the proper ritual?"

"Of course. There's no doubt about it. Uh—your whole life changes just from a mere meager moon festival. The lesser Sabbaths are *lunar* periods directly. The greater Sabbaths are *solar* positions. The reason I speak to you so freely is that I opened your book* and I was very pleased to see some references you made; you're absolutely correct. The position of a festival is not to be taken in a monotheistic sense. This is the date, and every time you come to that day, that's it. Any ancient priest of integrity always related to the positions of the heavens. It should be celebrated according to the movements of the stars and according to the rectification of the calendar. The greater Sabbaths are no longer on Hallowe'en, May Day, or Candlemas. They are at least a month away. They are on the solstices."

"In *your* calendar, what are the exact dates today in 1971?"

"They change according to the calculation of the year. Every year the calendar moves fifty-seven seconds. For example, the solstice takes place when the sun is in Sagittarius, approximately on December 21. But if you check it out in the astronomical calendar, you'll find that the sun is *not* in Capricorn; it is in the constellation of Sagittarius."

* *The Truth About Witchcraft.*

"For 1971, what are the major solstice holidays?"

"We haven't set up anything beyond the Blue Goddess Festival, which would be the twenty-first of March."

"What is the Blue Goddess?"

"You have never heard of the Blue Goddess? The most famous of all. You wear a thing around your neck which relates to her. The Blue Goddess is one of the most notorious of all deities. She is the lascivious goddess of fertility. She is also known as Astarte. In the metamorphosis of divinity, we have three words we use. The first one I've already told you: Sabbath. Sabbath is neither male nor female. We have its *reflection,* which we call *amn,* pronounced 'amoon.' This is the reflection, the delusion, in the great mirror. The third is the physical manifestation, the universe incarnate, what you call *nature.* This is Sybaris. The term *sybaritic* means a voluptuous effeminate. Sybaris, personified, is the physical manifestation of woman. When you have to identify something you do not *know,* you must use symbols. In symbols for the human being, the most primordial identity is *the woman.* A woman is born, and she identifies with where she comes from. It is always the mother, never the father, for you know who the mother is but very seldom even the mother knows who the father is. Thus the best symbol of physical creation is *woman.* Man is born of woman. This is the Great Mother Goddess or the White Goddess. She has four identities. The Aztecs identified them in the colors of the four points of the compass, as did the Egyptians with the four Isises. The White Goddess, which Robert Graves was able to identify, is one. The Blue Goddess is two, but in numerical sequence the Red Goddess is one, the White Goddess two, the Blue Goddess three, and the Yellow Goddess four."

"Can you give me the attributes of the four colors?"

"They represent the four races of man, and refer to the four points of the compass. Also, the cycle of life. Birth—the Red Goddess—the seed. Life is the White Goddess, the duality of illusion. The physical aspect is the Blue Goddess, related to fertility. Finally death, the Yellow Goddess."

"You mentioned that the festival of the Blue Goddess will be celebrated around the twenty-first of March."

"Very simply, the Red Goddess begins with the position of Virgo, that is to say, the autumnal equinox. *That* is the beginning of the year, though we celebrate the feast of Janus, the first day of January, because of the identity of the gods. The autumnal equinox marks the beginning of the calendar. We're going by the Babylonian system, in which the Blue Goddess festival was extremely important. From the 'ritual king' is derived, as you probably know, the so-called Black Mass with the business of lovemaking.

"But the idea of a *priest* is degenerate because a true priest is neither male nor female, but androgynous. I have been taught that the word *pontifex* means bridge because he's an in-between. In the word "babylou" *bab* means gate, *ylou* is the name of a god, so Babylon was the *gateway of the gods*.

"Everybody is so concerned with white and black magic, but the truth of the matter is that there is *no such thing* as white or black magic. There is no left or right. There is only one thing, one art—the art of metamorphosis. It is relative as to whether it is going to be good or bad. How many people have done evil trying to do good!"

"You mentioned to me that on February 25 you will have what you call an *eclipse*. What is an eclipse in your terms?"

"An eclipse is the movement of one body in front of another, changing its condition. Such as the moon going in front of the sun, or the earth going between the two. It relates to people as well. We identify man with the moon, and woman with the sun. The idea of the eclipse is *our form of marriage*. With Sabaeans, the main god was Sin, the god of the moon, always male, not female. The patriarchal changeover has placed things differently, but in our matriarchy, man is identified with the moon. In spite of woman having her periods according to lunar cycles, man identifies much more with the *nature* of the moon. He is polygamous, promiscuous, bisexual, and itinerant.

"Woman identifies herself with her mother, develops a sense of security, knowing where she comes from and that she is able to create.

"In the eclipse, when a *man and a woman*, or *two men*, or *two women*, or *whatever*, want to come together in relationship to the gods, they must go through a ceremony in which they call for the interference of the gods. A human being is a metamorphosis of spirit, which is sexless and can become male or female according to the needs of incarnation. Consequently, it is justifiable for a man to desire another man in a holy situation such as an eclipse, or a woman, a woman. According to our mythology, men and women come from a natural order of *one* which was split into two parts. Therefore the amalgamation of a male and female, or heterosexual marriage, is, of course, of a higher order. But it does not necessarily mean that the other combinations cannot achieve a solar or lunar eclipse, too."

"The eclipse you're having next month—is this between a man and a woman?"

"Yes. They're young people. We just had an eclipse last month of an older couple. It was very difficult, because part of the ceremony is that the husband has to rape the bride—that is, take her away by force. That's the ending of the festival, and it was very difficult. He couldn't do this, he had a bum leg. He was in his fifties, and she was in her late teens. They went through a *solar* eclipse. The eclipses differ among solar, lunar, and mercurial. You make the choice; the solar is to be termed in terms of years, the lunar in terms of months, and the mercurial in terms of weeks."

"You mean it lasts only that long?"

"Lasts as long as the gods have foretold."

"Well, are these *temporary* marriages?"

"That's right. Therefore there is no divorce!"

"Please describe the ceremony you are having."

"This month we're having a *lunar* eclipse. A solar eclipse is very ostentatious, very magnificent. The lunar is more itinerant. All animals used for the actual ceremony must be *sacrificed*. In other words, you don't just buy a dead animal to eat. They must be sacrificed properly, in proper ritual."

"Do you always use animals?"

"For sacrifice, no. Sometimes vegetables, because vegetables *feel*; therefore the cutting of a vegetable is as much a legitimate sacrifice as the cutting of an animal."

"Well, what do you use the *animal* for?"

"For food. The thing is that the food that you partake of is a communion with the gods. So the animal must be glorified. In other words, the whole purpose of the sacrifice is that the spirit of the animal is given due respect; to *raise* the spirit and in a magical operation to allow this *elemental* to rise to a position where it may perhaps lead to human incarnation. If you buy it in a store, it is just not *kosher*, you see!"

"What about the two participants?"

"There is a thirteen-day abstinence required from all physical contact between the two. The last day neither the male nor the female may look at the other. The bride goes into the fanum. We do not call them temples, because a temple is a *specifically dedicated* area, the *sanctum sanctorum*. No one enters, except the priests in relationship to the god. The little altar behind the veil, *that* is the temple. Fanum is where people *congregate*. There the bride is taught to make bread, so that if nothing else, she'll know how to make bread to sustain the relationship. The foods are begun to be prepared—except one. The one that relates to the actual ritual itself must be killed *during* the ritual.

"The ritual is divided into four parts, representing the four goddesses. The main thing is that the bride and groom are joined *as one*. They die, then immerse themselves in the *kiva*, meaning underground ceremonial chamber, and there through a ceremonial process call upon the God of Time. To know how long they should be together, the god Saturn is evoked. The female brings a glass, the male brings wine, and after the bread has been eaten and the wine drunk, and the proper ablutions and ceremonial things are done, the animal is sacrificed and the glass is broken. It is put inside of a linen wrapping. The *pontifex maximus*, the high priest, is leading the ceremonial. He makes a gesture like an inverted Y, and then moves his arms straight down, thus achieving an esoteric symbol of male and female joined, and at the same time achieving the destruction of the glass within the material. Then the *pontifex maximus* opens it and counts the pieces.

"If it is a lunar eclipse, you use silver rings; if it's a solar eclipse, you use gold rings. The ring you use is the *ring of the heart*. The right hand is the sun, and the left hand is the moon. The lower digit is emotion, and the upper digit is mature wealth. This is why you wear *two* rings. The one that you put down here is your engagement to the heart, and the other is the engagement to the material possessions, which is the final covenant of marriage.

"Then the pieces of glass in the material are counted. In a solar eclipse, the large pieces denote how many years, the medium-size pieces, how many months, the small pieces, how many weeks they will be together. With a lunar eclipse, the large pieces denote months, the medium-size pieces, weeks, and the small pieces, days. If it was a mercurial eclipse, the pieces denote weeks, days, and hours."

"You mean how long the marriage will *last?*"

"Right. At the same time, it tells you *how* the marriage is going to go. For the first three years you're going to have this or that, because of a certain way of inspecting the pieces. If halfway through you suddenly find that she's a slob or you can't stand her, you know that there's a time when it's going to all end; and you might suddenly find at the end of the eclipse that you really dig this chick, and you want to be reeclipsed—which you can do!"

"Beautiful," I said admiringly, for the system seemed to me to be far better than Reno.

"You must understand *from the very beginning* that you will part ways. If you do, it is magnificent. However, you must take into consideration in heterosexual relationships the possibility of a child. Consequently, you have godparents. If a person who is unpontifical is chosen, then there must be two—one of male and one of female sex. You can also choose a *pontifex maximus*, in which case only one is needed because he is considered to be of both sexes. Every *pontifex* must accept because if anything comes from this marriage, *he* is responsible. If the two parties split, and there is a child, and neither one can keep it, then it becomes a ward of the temple.

"When two people marry, neither one of them takes the other's name. You can choose your *ecliptical* name, and that is the name that you two go under, which is a third name, and when you break, the child born of the union is known under that name. That way, the individual does not belong to husband or wife, but to *himself*."

"In the ceremony, after the breaking of the glass, what follows?"

"Many things. Very briefly, in the first ceremony of the four, there is a veil between the bride and the groom. It is totally homosexual, as it is in the first stages of man's thought. That is, the females all go with the bride, and the males all go with the groom. In the outside world today you have the *metamorphosis* of what you call the *stag party*, and the *shower*."

"I gather there are large groups of people present."

"Of course. The husband and wife are separated because they are of their sex. If you have a *homosexual* marriage, then you separate them according to the individuals themselves, and their friends. During the ceremony they die, symbolically speaking. They're enveloped in a great veil, which leads them off to the *kiva*, the underground ceremonial chamber which no one goes into except the bride and the groom for their covenant with the divinity."

"How long are they underground?"

"Usually about an hour because you have to go through a whole ceremony, which is the rings, and the gods, and the sacrifice and everything else. But while they're there, the people go to the *get-har*, or "birth house"—that is, the bedroom, to decorate it. All the guests mingle, and meet each other. We have a temple orchestra. Then, when they come out, a small child, or a small person, leads, and everybody makes a great noise, to ward off evil spirits, because the couple is in a state of bliss. Barley and rice are thrown in their path; the child brings the wine into the *get-har*, and comes out with a torch and goes back down into the *kiva* and extinguishes it, carrying the life blood from the god over.

"Then the bride and groom are literally *thrown* into this bedroom, and the veil is rent from them. The doors are shut and closed. The bride and groom evoke the gods and then they make love as if for the very first time in their lives. Remember, the couple has abstained for thirteen days from any physical contact. There is food, there is perfume, and they talk, touch, and forget the gods, and *become one*.

"Outside the guests sing songs of love, dance, and evoke Venus, or the Blue Goddess, to bring about fertility."

"I gather the house is closed off from the rest of the temple?"

"Right. It is either another building altogether, or in our case, because we're limited, right next to it. Nobody goes in there, that is, the bride and groom are not seen by anybody from the second ceremony to the fourth."

"How are the people dressed for this ceremony?"

"The community is dressed comfortably. The bride and groom in special dress, which is rather *meager*. A loose garment is important; you do not have to be nude. A loose garment is sometimes better than nudity because you're creating electricity.

This is much more favorable than pure nudity, where there is nothing to rub unless you have bodies rubbing against each other."

"Is there more?"

"Certainly. We were only at the third ceremony."

"Do they emerge from the chamber?"

"At their convenience, which is generally about an hour later, they come out. They change into normal street wear, traveling clothes. When the door is opened, everybody goes in, there is singing of love songs, and everybody must worship the bride and groom as *gods,* and bring food to the door, and burn incense. If the bride and groom take too long, there's a point where the people storm the *get-har.* They must be finished by a certain time. It is not always told to them *when.* But if they're not finished, then they're pulled out. Then there is great jubilation and wild dancing in which you have the fourth goddess, the drunken one, the Yellow Goddess of great joy.

"They emerge not as a man and a wife, but together as part of *one,* you see; they're *one person* now. The table is brought, and communion of all people involved is made with the gods. The food the temple cooks have prepared is brought in by the pontifical order. All nine courses are exhibited, people eat, there is dancing, drinking, and everything.

"At a very specific time, which is premeditated by astrological computation and preset by the *pontifex,* the groom must end the ceremony. The way he ends it is by suddenly 'raping' the bride—that is, taking her away *by force.* He goes around to her, picks her up, runs around the table three times, and then goes right out. In the meantime, the people grab hold of rice, which the priest must have nearby, and throw it at them. There is great clamor and carrying on as they go away."

"Why is it necessary for the symbolic raping of the bride when they have already consummated the marriage?"

"Because it is the act of *motion,* not the act of rape or sex.

Sex itself is assumed to have taken place *before*. The point
of the rape relates to a magical ceremonial. Everything that
has been conjured and created there for the good of the bride
and groom must be taken by them. They must pull with them
as much of that force as they possibly can, and this can only
be done in the *symbolic act of rape*."

"How many members does your group have at the moment?"

"To be a Sabaean you do not have to belong to any particular
church or group. It is a state of mind."

"Is there a membership?"

"In order to belong to it, you go through what we call
esbats, which are meetings; you go to an open meeting, and
then eventually to closed meetings, until finally you achieve
moon festivals—certain moon festivals—and then after those
moon festivals you finally go into the solar festivals and you're
in. But it makes a difference how initiated an individual is.
The individual must relate to the group. If an individual doesn't
quite fit with the *rest of the group*, then you cannot create
the homogeneity that you need to have."

"Do you have restrictions, as with witchcraft, to thirteen
members?"

"We do not. We have invited as many as a hundred people,
and as few as twenty. Somehow the gods seem to make the
choice; we do not. The number generally comes to around
twenty-one, or twenty-two."

"You yourself are a high priest?"

"No, I am the Rex Sacrorum. The high priest is the priest
who rules a ceremony; it could be any *pontifex*."

"You are above that? You are the head of the organization?"

"Yes. We have a state charter."

"Are there other groups like yours?"

"I was the first one in Illinois. I have no contact with any
others."

"This philosophy did not originate entirely with you, then?"

"It is a tradition I am *following*; its roots are in the Megalithic

Period in Spain, pre-Celtic; connected also with the Mesopotamian priesthood."

"How old were you when you came here?"

"That I never divulge! I was born in Europe, and I have gone to school there, in Spain and different places in Europe, in the West Indies, in Cuba, and in the United States."

"I hope," he added, "you will not judge Sabaeanism by my person alone. In the past I know that I have appeared to mislead people as to my character. Sabaeanism is a philosophy of earth and must include all that is on it. To exclude *anything* is unnatural."

With a flourish, he wrapped his long woolen scarf around his neck and left.

*

Unfortunately, I could not attend the lunar eclipse on February 25, 1971, since I had a previous engagement in Washington, D.C. Some other time I am sure I will be able to witness in person one of Frederic de Arechaga's rituals, for we parted friends.

Shortly after our meeting, I found myself in Hollywood during a lunar eclipse—a real one up in the sky. As I peered at the moon and noticed the dark shadows creeping slowly but surely over her silvery face, I couldn't help feeling that Frederic's kind of eclipse was probably a lot less menacing. But I still can't get used to the idea that the moon is not a lady.

*

If it strikes you as strange that the gods of ancient Egypt, Greece, and Rome should be resurrected by worshipers in the 1970's in sophisticated America, stop for a moment and think: Isn't Christianity based upon the philosophy and life of a man who lived in ancient Judea two thousand years ago? Doesn't much of the Far East look to a deified prophet who trod the earth six hundred years before the Christian era? What is time to the gods? Spiritual truth is timeless.

BOOK FOUR

THE MASTERS OF MAGIC

"True magic is an act of love. It contributes to your becoming what you are, and it is part of the cosmic law and will. In this respect it is the true religion. Magic respects the will to exist and the right to exist of every creature and renounces if at all possible all rituals requiring blood sacrifice." Thus postulates Dr. Klingsor, adept and author of *Experimental Magic*.

Magic to the average person means stage manipulation, the skill of the prestidigitator, sleight of hand, an art of elusion and definitely nothing real. The word itself is derived from *magus*, which has an entirely different meaning. The magi of old were adept wise men capable of harnessing the forces of nature in a way the average person was unable to. It is a curious irony that modern magicians both professional and amateur are by and large the most skeptical of all people when it comes to the acceptance of psychic phenomena. I have never yet met a magician who wasn't hell bent trying to disprove everything any serious researcher had ever discovered in the field of extrasensory perception. Sometimes stage magicians go to extreme ends of reasoning to satisfy themselves that there really isn't anything to psychic research. I can understand

such an attitude on the part of people who have been trained
to imitate many things in a way that looks miraculous, even
impossible, and contrary to natural law. Consequently, they
feel they can imitate everything else, too. Nothing could be
further from the truth, of course. But we are not discussing
that kind of magic. Not the cheap parlor tricks with cards,
handkerchiefs, rabbits pulled out of hats, and the somewhat
more daring stage trick of removing the shorts from an un-
suspecting member of the audience who has volunteered to
come up and be surprised.

Wicca, the old witchcraft tradition, uses magic to make
things happen. In this respect magic is simply the detailed
and advanced understanding of the laws of nature beyond that
which the average person knows. With this little-known knowledge or advanced information, the witch practicing magic also
creates a kind of performance. What the witch or shaman or
priest does seems miraculous to the average member of the
community since he cannot understand it. But here the sim-
ilarity with stage magic ends. While the modern magician produces an illusion, witchcraft magic delivers the real thing. Every
manipulation of people or things seemingly in circumvention
of orthodox or natural law is actually happening. These are
not supernatural doings, but they appear to be to the un-
initiated. When a man in love speaks of the magic emanating
from the subject of his affections as the causative factor of
his curious state of being, he simply acknowledges that something strange has happened to him for which he cannot account
by logical means. He can't put his finger on it and yet it is very
real to him. Consequently, it is magic. Magic is one of the
three basic elements in the Old Religion, the other two being
ritual and belief in reincarnation. But not all magic in the
narrow sense of the term occurs in the covens of Wicca.

The line from witchcraft into the Masonic lodges of today
passes by many strange and secret societies, cults, religious
groups sometimes called covens, sometimes called lodges or

even churches. They all have one basic tenet in common: the inner rites must remain secret. Only initiates may know certain key phrases or facts about the group. Secrecy is necessary, from the group's point of view, not only to protect the potency of their ritual, but also to keep the teachings from being profaned through indiscriminate discussion, dissemination, or publication. There is nothing democratic about pagan movements in the sense in which we understand the term today politically. To be sure, all are equal within a coven or group, but knowledge must be earned through study. Initiation must proceed by degrees, and the outsider is not as good as the initiate. Nor is the initiate from another group as good as the one from one's own. Sometimes these distinctions are arbitrary, snobbish, or just foolish. But they have given the members of some very secret groups strength through the ages and have helped preserve their heritage unspoiled and apparently intact.

*

In Pasadena, California, there is a group calling itself O.T.A., which stands for Order of the Temple of Astarte. Lest this conjure up visions of lascivious services in honor of the love goddess, let me assure you that the O.T.A. is a hermetic order which practices "magick" in the Western mystical tradition. "Hermetic" is a term derived from Hermes and goes back to the first and second century of our era, when a new philosophy based largely upon Greek and late Egyptian ideas came into fashion. Basically, hermetism teaches that "the human soul can only escape from its bondage to matter if it possesses the true knowledge or understanding (gnosis), which is the privilege of a select few," according to Olof Gigon in *Man, Myth and Magic*.

The hermetic reaches out to God through mystical experience. If man extends himself beyond bodily limits and the limitations of space and time by certain rituals, he will know God. This, then, is essentially an intellectual approach to liberation and oneness with the deity by the use of the path of mysticism.

O.T.A. practices the entire spectrum of what they refer to as "high magick," but they do not engage themselves in the practice of so-called black magic or anything that might have harmful results. Much of their ritual is kabbalistic, an amalgamation of the ancient Hebrew mystic traditions, evocation of demons in the medieval manner, and the hermetic ideals.

There doesn't seem to be much of Astarte in the group, at least not the way I know the lady. O.T.A. is closely allied with the Church of the Hermetic Sciences, a nonprofit organization with a proper license to practice religion. Members of the group pay dues, and nonmembers usually make a donation when they attend one of the functions.

There are classes teaching the concepts of the lodge and some of them are open to the public. Their literature is available from Box 3341, Pasadena, California. In this literature they warn potential members that drugs are out, and any past or current affiliation with extremist political or satanist organizations is equally frowned upon. "We are a basically religious order, but we do not require our students to believe that which we believe," they explain. The brotherhood, as it likes to be called, has some very artistic stationery and even more artistic headquarters, which was once a church belonging to the Aimée Semple McPherson sect.

All of the artistic work and the theories behind this brotherhood are the brainchild of an extremely talented young man by the occult name of Frater Aleyin. He is aided and abetted by another young man named Frater Khedemel, a part-time teacher and peace officer. At present the O.T.A. numbers, besides these two leaders, about six other people, half of them women and all of them very young. Everyone has a fraternity name, of course, and as soon as they are assembled inside their temple they address each other only by these fanciful names, most of which are derived from the Arabic or Indian languages.

"We are competent young men and women engaged in a supreme adventure, not disillusioned misfits looking for mutual support in collective pseudo-religious sublimation," the master explained to me at our first meeting while he was driving me back from Pasadena to my Hollywood hotel. None of the people in his group are shiftless or out of work, it is true. They go to great pains to differentiate between their activities and direction and that of the Wicca and other pagan groups. They are not witches, they assert, and they are perfectly right. They are not witches, but they are pagans, although they would prefer to think of themselves as "pre-Christian" rather than pagan.

When I expressed an interest in coming to an actual ritual on my next trip to California, O.T.A. invited me not only to come and be part of one, but also to return and film an excerpt for my forthcoming documentary on the pagan religions.

*

Prior to my arrival in Los Angeles at the end of January 1971, I was sent a schedule of activities and operations that would have done a military commander in Vietnam proud. As a matter of fact, Frater Aleyin was a captain in the Green Berets at one time, although I suspect that his political views nowadays are of a less military character.

The schedule was full of words like "operations," "sixteen thirty hours," "maximum attendance requested"—the only thing missing was the phrase "travel orders." It is not surprising to find so much imagination expended on this project. The master is not only a capable artist, but he also writes science fiction. He's a man of much knowledge and many words.

"Magick is the 'art' which seeks to develop the spark of divinity in the individual human spirit. It is also the occult science of knowing yourself from the dawn of time up to and including your present karmic and ancestral personality," he explained.

On February 4, 1971, I was to find out for myself what exactly the O.T.A. kind of magic was like. The boys picked me up at my hotel, and as early as 7 P.M. we arrived at the temple in Pasadena. This gave me ample time to look around and inspect the premises. One enters the temple through a hall, in the center of which is a low table. Around that table the members squat or sit and discuss the affairs of the brotherhood.

The walls are covered with scrolls containing quotations from mystic literature, a set of swords, and a number of very attractive paintings from the brush of the master himself.

In an adjoining room, which is somewhat larger than the first one, the inner temple has been established. Painted in black, it is illuminated by stage lights in various colors that give it an almost psychedelic effect. In the center there is a circle consisting of a slightly raised narrow wooden platform. Farther back outside the circle there is a gong, and facing forward just outside the circle, a large mirror on a stand. When I first inspected the temple that mirror was covered, since it played a major part in the ritual that was to follow shortly.

By eight o'clock everyone had arrived and changed into his costume. The proper attire for the O.T.A. rituals, at least for most of them, appears to be a simple black robe. The robe consists of a long piece of black cloth with a hole cut for the head. It is held together by a piece of cord. Under the robe nothing else is worn, but sandals are allowed since the floor is cold. I had arranged to have a robe made up for me so I could join in the ritual of the evening.

There were seven of us now in the outer hall, chatting informally. I asked the master to explain the nature of tonight's "operation."

"We will try to conjure up the spirit of Baal," he explained earnestly. "Baal is a king and he has that rank. He lives in the East and rules over an invisible realm of eternal spirits. He appears in diverse shapes, sometimes like a cat, sometimes like a toad, and sometimes like a man, and sometimes in all these forms at once. He speaks hoarsely. This is his character."

He then showed me a number of rare books in which the various demons of the medieval tradition were listed by name, occupation, job preference, and abode; their faces and shapes were also shown. About the only thing missing was their telephone numbers, but then demons *wouldn't* use the telephone even if it had been invented in the Middle Ages.

*

If I sound facetious, I do not mean to be. Demonology has a definite role to play in the art of evocation. So long as the magician realizes that the spirit or deity he is evoking is a symbolic representation of a principle represented also within himself in some fashion, he is merely expressing the laws of nature in a somewhat fanciful and romantic manner. But when the demons of the various realms become flesh-and-blood people with supernatural abilities and when these realms are described like historical kingdoms, I find myself in a quandary. A careful study of the so-called grimoires or keys to demonology and magic shows an absolutely unlimited array of demons, spirits, rulers of various spheres—all of them with fanciful names and possessed of specific powers.

I think the danger of self-delusion is always present when esoteric concepts are vulgarized into three-dimensional representatives. How easy it is, then, for a superficial observer, such as a Hollywood motion-picture producer, to create a film showing the struggle of a serious researcher with demonology as if there were indeed such dangers, deadly dangers, from the demon Asmodius, a very naughty fellow. Demons and elementals, or nature spirits, are not devils. We already know that the devil in terms of Christianity is a fanciful invention. The devil within all of us is another matter. That one is very real at times, and so are the demons that live both without and within our world. One must never forget that magical evocation encourages the practice of imagination, creating from within oneself and projecting onto the outside. To work it the other way around, that is, to draw objectively existing demons into one's orbit, is another matter.

*

Presently the master returned resplendent in a different kind of robe. Just like the others, he wore a hood over his head, but there was a large rose cross on his chest, and in his hand he carried a two-pointed spear, his mace of office as master. The time was at hand, and one by one we followed him into the other room. After we had all taken our positions inside and outside the great circle, the gong was struck by Frater Khedemel and the ritual began.

For about two minutes the congregation intoned the vowels I E A O U in deep, sonorous voices, while walking around the magic circle. The letters stand for the name of God. I took my place just inside the circle with my back toward the master, looking straight toward the great mirror, which was now uncovered. The glass became visible in the dim candlelight.

I was to "scrye" in the great mirror—to do some crystal gazing in the hope that Baal might appear to me. "This I've got to see," I thought. Not because I would be frightened if Baal did appear, but because I was really looking forward to it. It sounded like an exciting trip into the land of mental adventures.

The master then thrust two long candlesticks into my hands and motioned me to hold them up so that I could see the mirror more clearly. What I saw was merely my face, but in time I might conceivably see someone lurking behind me. I honestly hoped I would, but I did not expect this to happen immediately. Projections of the mind do occur, and the strange feeling of the room, the heavy incense which rose from beneath my face, the gong, the voices of the participants—all these things might conceivably induce such a phenomenon within me.

The incense was of a special kind which I had never encountered before. It turned out to be a mixture peculiar to the

O.T.A. Seated on the floor just below me was one of the young girls who acted as assistant priestess. She kept feeding the incense burner with such fervor that my eyes began to water. Every time I moved my head to avoid being asphyxiated, I heard the concerned master whisper, "Are you all right, Hans?" I assured him that I was and he began his solemn invocations. After some conjurations in kabbalistic Hebrew, the four archangels were invoked to stand guard in front of the circle, in back of the circle, to the right and left of the circle. This corresponds to the invocation of the four quarters or the Ancient Ones of Wicca. Much of this material may be found in *The Book of Ceremonial Magic* by Arthur Edward Waite, a classic of the occult. But this is to my knowledge the only instance in recent American practice that the principles, rituals, incantations, and symbols of the kabbalah have been employed by a group of respectable and serious worshipers.

When properly understood, ceremonial magic, amulets, symbolisms, and even the names of the protective entities can be of real value in magical evocations or incantations. These are not scribblings or fantasy drawings made by self-deluded superstitious people. To the contrary, they are the work of scholars and true magicians in centuries past. When I expressed apprehension as to the proper use of demonology in our time, I was referring to the plane of existence of these principles rather than to their effectiveness, which I do not doubt.

Now the master started to summon Baal to "come from whatever part of the world you are in and answer our questions. Manifest that which we desire . . . presently . . . we summon thee in the name of —— . . . and thy mother, Ashtarot . . . we summon thee by thy middle name Tetragrammaton. . . ."

For about fifteen minutes the master repeated the invocation summoning the apparently still unwilling spirit of Baal to manifest. At first gently, later somewhat more threateningly, he commanded Baal to appear. The tone of his voice, the atmosphere of the temple, and me standing there with two

lighted candles and arms outstretched in front of the mirror
were pure magic in its theatrical application. As I stood there
staring into the half-darkened mirror, I thought *I felt* some
sort of presence hovering over my shoulder. I did not see the
clearly defined face of King Baal next to me in the glass, but
I felt *something*.

The following night the O.T.A. demonstrated a communion
service, and I was able to film some of it. This time the master
was dressed in a white robe really resplendent with his rose
cross and the various paraphernalia of his office.

The communion itself was as beautiful as any communion
service I've ever witnessed in church. Bread and salt were
used, with crackers taking the place of bread. Each communicant stepped up and was given these symbolic foods. The
master stood on the right side of the circle and his assistant
priestess stood on the left. Communicants moved around the
circle in such a way that communion took place simultane-
ously on both sides, giving it the feeling of a round robin or
continual ceremony.

The main difference between this communion and the one
usually found in church was the kiss male communion giver
bestowed upon female communicant and vice versa. With all
this kissing and the candlesticks and swords and robes I can
readily see why O.T.A. serves a useful and inspirational purpose in our drab world of materialism and disillusion. Perhaps
the magic of the O.T.A. is more intrinsic than even the master
realizes.

*

If I ever had any doubts that the Masters really existed in
the nonphysical world and that these were people with superior
knowledge and powers, I no longer feel that way. Too many
things have happened that could not be explained other than
by carefully planned and executed interference from beyond by
individuals of great wisdom and skills. Apparently, some of

their planning is long-range. They seek out people to carry their messages forward, bring them together when their ends can be better used in unison, and in general pull the strings. Anyone who believes he is master of his fate should ponder this. We are all masters of our decisions which determine the next step, but opportunities and situations are thrown our way for reasons, and not haphazardly.

It appears to me from what I have learned that those on the other side of life possessed of superior knowledge, wisdom, and importance are permitted free rein in guiding humanity on earth in such a way that humanity becomes aware of higher values and thus redeems itself in time. The living then become the pawns of the spiritual entities within the limitations of nature; that is to say, nothing may be forced upon a flesh-and-blood person, but situations can be manipulated so that the selected individual can make his or her choice. If the Masters have played their cards right and picked the proper individuals they will very likely make the kind of choice that will carry out the Masters' plan. I haven't the slightest idea who the supervisor of all this is, but there must be a well-regulated system as to what the Masters are permitted to do and what they are not. It seems also to involve karmic values and relationships, and it is by no means a free interchange of ideas from the beyond through willing individuals on earth.

In retrospect, I am fully convinced that the meeting between Alice McDermott and me had been arranged many years before while each one of us was still undergoing certain training and did not know of each other. The ultimate purpose was to bring across the veil the knowledge possessed by certain Masters or wise teachers, and in particular one known in his earth life as Nicholas Roerich.

Mr. Roerich was a great mystic and superb painter who lived most of his life in India and Tibet, rarely visiting the United States, his native country. Long after he had passed away in the 1930's, his admirers and disciples erected to him a monument in the form of a skyscraper, which contained a gallery and lecture hall. This is now known as the Master Institute and is at the corner of 103rd Street and Riverside Drive. Only the name and the art displayed in the corridors as well as the museum downstairs point out the connection with Nicholas Roerich.

The building itself is run as an expensive apartment house; most of the tenants are intellectuals from nearby Columbia University or foreign government officials. Once in a while an artist also finds space in this beautiful building.

Some years ago, after a series of quarrels between the latter-day admirers of the great Roerich, a split developed, and a second Roerich gallery and museum was opened at 319 West 107th Street.

Long before I had ever heard of Alice McDermott, I was walking up Riverside Drive in search of an apartment. This was in the late 1950's, and apartments were not easy to get. Suddenly I found myself in front of the Master Institute at the corner of 103rd Street. I went inside and within a matter of minutes had found exactly what I was looking for. My late father and I shared a penthouse apartment on the nineteenth floor of this building for several years. It was then that I began to learn for the first time of Roerich's work. I wonder if I wasn't directed there to gaze at the mystical paintings found on every floor!

Three years later, in *Ghost Hunter*, my first book dealing with psychic phenomena, I was able to include a brief report of a haunting at the very building in which I was then living. I did not realize that there was underneath my feet a room where the spirit of Nicholas Roerich had appeared to a Miss Roland during a lecture dealing with his favorite topic, mysticism. At the time I wrote of this story, I tried in vain to get confirmation of it from the owners of both Roerich buildings.

I moved from the Master Institute building in 1962 and have not been back since.

*

But, unknown to me, Roerich was planning things. Four years later, in 1966, he apparently made his next move. That year he arranged for Alice McDermott, then about nineteen years old, to contact me concerning her psychic experiences. At the time, of course, I had no inkling of this, and only now, in retrospect and with all the material in my hands, am I able to see Nicholas Roerich's fine hand.

Alice has had psychic experiences all her life. One of the more memorable occasions involved a car accident which she correctly foresaw, and which might have harmed her mother. Since she could not convince her mother of her powers, Alice managed to take the more exposed seat when they entered the car. The accident did occur just as she had predicted, but because she had changed seats, her mother was not hurt and Alice had only whiplash.

The reason she got in touch with me was a somewhat frightening experience she had had at the Cafe Bizarre in Greenwich Village, New York. The cafe is located in what used to be Aaron Burr's stables, and on a casual visit there with friends, she had actually experienced his presence. She managed to draw the face of a man with piercing black eyes whom she had seen, and I was able to show that it was indeed Aaron Burr. At the time of her experience, Alice had no idea that the cafe had anything to do with him.

Another psychic experience occurred while she was a postulant in a Long Island monastery. She saw the ghostly figure of a woman, who was later identified as the daughter of a former owner of the estate which is now the monastery.

At the time of our initial meetings, it was clear to me that Alice was an exceptionally gifted psychic who might very well develop further powers as time went on. Accordingly, I encouraged her to get in touch with me if anything extraordinary should happen to her. Somehow I had the vague feeling that we would meet again, but several years passed and I heard nothing further from her.

Then in January 1970 I received a phone call from her. She wanted to see me on a matter of some concern to her, and we met again in my study. In the intervening years, Alice had become involved with certain aspects of yoga.

"This group," she explained, "taught one how to find one's higher self, and to achieve oneself *through* the higher self, make a better life on earth, and to fulfill one's karma without making new karma for oneself."

"What sort of work did you undertake when you were part of that group?" I asked.

"Meditation and reading once a week."

"Did you ever have any experience of ecstasy or trance or anything like an out-of-the-body experience while meditating in yoga class?"

"Yes. I did."

"Did at any time an entity—a personality other than a living person—make contact with you?"

"Yes, during one of the classes. Nicholas Roerich. He came to me, but he did not mention his name. He was dressed in a long white robe. He informed me that he was here to teach me. That was in October of 1969."

"Had other spirit entities approached you during the yoga classes?"

"No, no one else."

"Did you see or hear him?"

"It was during meditation that I saw him."

"Did anyone else present see him?"

"Yes, one of the men. Not physically, but in meditation."

"How many were there in the group at that time?"

"There were eleven present that night. I didn't just say *who* it was; I described him, and our descriptions agreed with one another. Sylvia, the head of the group, showed me a number of pictures so I could identify him. Those were the ones that she had of the Seven Masters. And one of the pictures was of the man I had seen, Nicholas Roerich."

"You had never seen a picture of this man before?

"Never!"

"What did he wear in the picture?"

"He was dressed in oriental attire. In my meditation experience he wore a long white robe and it had a belt on the side."

"Had you ever heard of Roerich before you joined this group?"

"No."

"In the books that you read in the yoga class, how was he described?"

"He wasn't described at all; only his writings were mentioned, *Morea's Garden*, Book I and Book II, and *Agni Yoga*."

"What exactly did he tell you?"

"He said he would teach me *the ways*. He said that I must trust him, have faith in him, and he would help me in my everyday life besides my *other life*."

"When was the next time you had any contact with this entity?"

"The following night I dreamed of him. He started to teach me. He wore the same white robe again."

"What did he teach you on this second occasion?"

"He gave me an amulet. He showed it to me and said, Write it down. It was a round copper disc on a chain. He said, Copy these letters, write them down, and have one made up."

"Did you?"

"Yes."

"What did it look like?"

"I never saw the writing before; I was not familiar with it. It wasn't English. He came back again a couple of days later. And he gave me my initial. He said that in a past life I had achieved a certain status, and I had an initial, and I was to keep this initial for my name."

"Did you recognize it?"

"No, I didn't."

"What was the next step?"

"Then I received writings. He would say, Sit down and write. Sometimes he'd wake me up in my sleep and tell me that you have to write now."

"You heard him, too?"

"Yes."

"Did your husband hear him?"

"No."

"What did you do?"

"I'd go outside the bedroom and write for a while. I put the pen down, I would find my hands getting itchy, and I'd *have* to pick it up again. When I was finished, I knew it. If I wanted to stop writing, he wouldn't let me."

"How many times did he come to you after that?"

"Dozens of times."

"What was the essence of the material he dictated to you?"

"Magic. He said clear, unadulterated magic."

"Did he identify himself to you as Roerich?"

"Never."

"Then you only know that it was he from the photograph? Did you ever question him about who he was?"

"I did, and he just smiled. I said, now I *know* who you are. He just smiled."

"How did you speak to him?"

"By telepathy."

"When he spoke of magic to you, did he tell you what you should do with this knowledge?"

"He told me that I should share it with the world; that it's for the world to know, not only for me."

"Have you yourself ever applied any of this magic?"

"There was a man who kept sending me psychic vibrations,

and trying to hurt me psychically. Roerich told me, Make a circle, put his name in it, write these letters around it, and burn three red candles for three days. I did it, and from that day on I have had no problems with this man."

"On what other occasions did you use magic taught you by this Master?"

"Burning candles mostly, if there was sickness in the house. I was given a chart of different colored candles to use for different things. Green, for money and security; blue, to ward off evil; red has to do with sexual desires, but it also can call up the strongest vibrations within you, and raise them up, and make you work better. Black is to call upon the dead; and white is for purification."

"Was anything else to be done while these candles were being burned? Was there any particular rite?"

"Sandalwood incense, and a silver bell had to be rung three times."

"Did he ever tell you to appeal to any particular deity?"

"Yes. *Diana*. I was supposed to—submit myself unto you, I submit myself unto you as your daughter; enlighten me and teach me."

"Did you ever share the messages you received from Roerich with the group?"

"Sometimes. It depended on his instructions."

"What other magic did he teach you?"

"If somebody were bothering me, he told me to get a silver-colored box with red lining and burn a piece of paper with their name on it inside, keep it closed, and then scatter it to the four winds within twelve days."

"Who do you think is the deity that helps you?"

"I think Diana."

"How would you define Diana?"

"I think she is part of a whole energy force; these deities are part of a great body, working different branches in different ways, but to attain *one* goal."

"Did Roerich tell you to work with others outside of the yoga group?"

"Yes; he told me to come to *you*."

"Is he present as you speak?"

"Yes; now there is something coming through about *blessing the circle*. You go around the circle in a clockwise manner. He is blessing the circle with incense."

"Is there anything else used—I mean other tools, other elements?"

"Yes, but that's 'of the old way.'"

"How does the *new* way differ from the *old* way?"

"There'll be no steel present; no metal."

"Is there one who leads?"

"The Avatar."

I decided to leave the ceremonial material for the moment. "Prior to your interest in this yoga group," I asked, "did you have any interest in witchcraft, magic, the esoteric—outside of ESP and the experiences you yourself had had?"

"Not really."

"Have you read a great deal about it?"

"No."

"In your own family, is there a background in psychic phenomena?"

"No."

"Has Roerich ever taken you astrally out of the body, while asleep, to certain places?"

"Yes: a cave with an altar in it; there were candles around it. People began to come in, all dressed in white. He put me in front of the altar and said, Now you will bless these things and you will do as I tell you. I was standing on the side at first, and then I was told to come to the center. On the altar there were old books—the writing wasn't English. There was chanting in the background."

"What was done with you at that point in the dream?"

"There was an incense burner, similar to the ones used in

the Catholic Church, and I was blessed with the incense; my hands were bound after that, with white cord, around the wrists. Then oil was put on my forehead, and something bitter was given to me to drink; I could taste it when I woke up. Roerich held the cup and gave it to me. It was like a stone cup. It was round, and the liquid in the cup was green. Then he took it and placed it back on the altar. He was wearing a white robe. He unbound my hands and put them on top of the book, palms down; then he turned them around and put the backs down, then he blessed both hands with some sort of sign, also with the balm."

"Did he speak?"

"He was saying something to me, in a foreign language, then he gave me a white candle. I had to hold the candle and read the book, but it wasn't *my* voice coming forth; and I couldn't really read it, but I *was* reading it! It wasn't *my* voice, but it was *me!*"

"Did you have this dream vision just once?"

"No, on several occasions, in different caves. One time a lamb was sacrificed. But no blood came from the lamb. The lamb was not killed; it was just a symbolism; the lamb was young, very small. Another time all sorts of herbs were being blessed; they were not like the herbs that you buy but in their full form still, like a plant.

"Did you see others participating in these rites?"

"Sometimes three or four would do things around the altar, but the main group would stay back and chant."

"Men and women?"

"No women. There was one ritual I recall, where I was told I had to walk through fire. I walked through the fire, and yet, every time I touched the fire it was ice-cold. Then I had to sit down, and drink from the fountain near the fire, and eat from a table nearby. Everything was surrounded by fire, yet it was cold to the touch."

"When you woke up, did you feel different?"

"I felt like I was cleansed."

"How do rituals, such as the ones Roerich showed you, relate to today's problems?" I finally asked.

"Today, people put too much emphasis on life and not enough on spirit. The energy they bring forth is not of the spirit but of the body."

"Can the energy of the body be used positively if guided by proper thought?"

"There is not enough emphasis upon the spirit. It should be understood by those that practice paganism that the spirit and body are equal; the spirit not less than the body, nor the body less than the spirit. Being normal, mortal creatures, people will look only to the body. Body and spirit must go together, so they can reach the greater goals. There are forces present here upon earth which may solve many of the world's problems. They are people who have learned to use their bodies and souls together in harmony. They are not known to the general public; they have normal jobs; they lead normal lives. But in times of crisis they unite and meet."

*

From then on in I saw Alice once a week for several months in succession. After some initial conversation, during which I tried to relax her and record whatever impressions, psychic feelings, or interesting visions she might have had between our meetings, I hypnotized her and eventually sent her back into previous lives. It is a moot point whether some of the knowledge displayed by her in hypnotic trance is actually the memory of one or several people who lived and died in centuries past and whose memories somehow are buried deep within the entity now living in New York City as Alice McDermott, or whether Alice's own unconscious when entranced is capable of collecting this information and projecting it to me.

What is important and remarkable is the fact that the information is not available to Alice in her ordinary life. I am satisfied that she has not undertaken detailed research from published sources, simply because the way in which she ties certain esoteric facts together makes sense only from the point of view of earlier incarnations as a witch or priestess of Diana, combined, stored up, and reiterated in her present self. This will become clearer as I report some of the material that has come through Alice's entranced lips.

*

Why would a twenty-four-year-old girl, tall, blond, and beautiful, mentally active, with a busy family life and hardly lacking in attention, subject herself to hours of travel from her home in Brooklyn, to weekly sessions on the couch during which she is clearly someone else she does not remember on awakening, unless there was a compelling, overriding motive or perhaps a mission beyond choice involved? Alice derived no financial benefit from her work with me. Probably the only reward she will attain out of the time we spent together is the sure knowledge of the Master's hand at her shoulder and the feeling that she is indeed fulfilling something of great importance. Only those who have had absolute proof of being guided by higher intelligence can appreciate such a statement. Then, too, of course, there is the resulting self-realization of her own person as Alice, and last, but possibly not least, my close and continuing friendship.

I had agreed to include the teachings of the Masters as they came to Alice from her particular Master, Nicholas Roerich, in my forthcoming book on the new pagans. I asked her to gather up all the notes she had made prior to our meeting, and the following week she turned over to me a number of observations, incantations, and strange drawings, which had been dictated to her by her mentor. This material came to Alice between October 27, 1969, and February 19, 1970. It was after the latter time that she was instructed to try to have much of it published. The style of these messages, the magic alphabet used, the symbolism of the amulets drawn, are totally alien to Alice McDermott's own personality and knowledge. I was able to research them only with difficulty and in some instances could not find a referred-to amulet in existing sources. In these cases I was confronted with a combination of several valid factors creating new combinations in a manner that only a great adept could have thought of.

I am now convinced that that adept was and is Master Nicholas Roerich. The following is the material received by Alice McDermott and transcribed from her original notes:

*

On November 10, 1969, she was given a spell for the purpose of subjecting another person to one individual's will. This is not so much a love spell as a power incantation.

This man is mine
I draw the powers of the sea and air
the flame is mine. I send thee strength of almighty
God. I am one with him.

Klim Hum.

Long time short time all time is mine.

I strip thee of thy foulness. Be thou mine. Open and I shall seek the good.

Rabuco—Rabuco—this man shall do unto me as I wish, as I desire, he shall feel me as he. I shall be part of him. He shall do my will—Rabuco—Rabuco.

This man shall do unto me.
This man shall do unto me.

I seek not evil, I will the good for all. This man shall do unto me unto me. He is mine and mine shall he be. He shall do unto me.

Black is black and white is white I am all white let you know that.

I am thee and thee are me. You shall feel the force of me.

Some of the words in Alice's transcripts are obviously kabbalistic terms and names. They are given here in the same phonetic
spelling she has put down on paper.

A group of spells against illness was given to her a short
time later:

Fire Air Water—come upon me draw out the foulness in me
banish the affliction of pain. Rest me mother earth.
Make me free of the pain I feel

Hel ze ack Hel ze ack make me free of the pain I feel

Eyes eyes eyes open wide see right and left see good and
bad eyes eyes eyes look to the stars for what you seek.

> Melz a buckta
> Melz a buckta make them well to see again

Fatness hunger there is no pain sweetness of heavens must
be for thee   Racel Racel do this for me.

There is a strange intermixture of kabbalistic Hebrew words
with Indian and Tibetan expressions. They are used not as the
central focal point of the incantations, but rather as outer
framework. While the emotional message of the spells seems
written in very good poetic English, clearly the work is of a
sophisticated, well-educated person. Sandalwood has to be
burned and candles lit while these spells or incantations are
being recited. Here are some of the more interesting ones.

To bring one's husband home

The wind be sweet, the
wind be strong, it brings
my loved one home to me.

He wanders not,
his guide be the light
he comes home to me.

To keep a man faithful

Love me only,
Love me as I love you
Seek not others be blind
to them.

I am thy sight, you see
only me, no others.

Love me only as I love you.

To remove depression

Fill thy heart with
thoughts of happiness.
Rays of love be transmitted

Racel—Racel—assist
in my quest of happiness.

To please a man

Fire of Light
Fire of Love
let him see
that which he wants

Fire of light
Fire of love
let him see that
which he wants.

To make things grow

I am one with nature
Grow plant thy leaves reach out for the
sky thy branches are filled with fruit.

I feed you will. I feed you love
You shall grow.

Na ha ra-na ha ra you shall grow.

To heal others

Open up I shall enter thee.
The Spirits shall mingle and
live as one. Michael the servant
assist me send the ray of healing.
I am the instrument.

Alice was informed that the notes she was taking would
be partially in English and partially in "an old language no
longer in use." She was made to write down strange letters
and symbols. The Hebrew letters "aleph" and "gimel," she was
told, had certain vibrations which would send forth healing.
Other letters were in "celestial script," and the combination of
certain letters and words in these strange alphabets would create
great power for those using them correctly. Of course, all amulets must be specifically made for a person to be effective, so
her name is often included among the symbols in the drawings
of amulets she was given by her mentor. One amulet given her
for protection in general has the following words written around
the outer edge: "Elohim adonay elyon elohe tetragramaton
sabaoth." As any student of the Kabbalah and of medieval
magic knows, these are various forms of names used for the
Deity.

While one could explain Alice's knowledge of the Tibetan
prayer formula "Om mani padni hum" by her association
with an Agni yoga group, this would certainly not apply to the
Hebrew terms and letters she also seems to be eminently familiar with. Her sole association with Judaism is the fact that
she once attended a seder, at which she recognized some of the

writing as Hebrew, letters she had been given previously by her mentor.

On another occasion she was given a formula for calling upon an angel for assistance. Four pentagrams are drawn in the four corners of a sheet of paper while the center is filled with the word "racel" written twice in order to form a cross. Thus the central letter "c" belongs to both words. Another amulet useful for protection consists of a circle within which the word "pax" is placed four times next to four crosses. In the very center of the circle the name of the individual to be protected is placed. Outside the circle the word "shanti" is written four times and in the corners four pentagrams are drawn. Both "shanti" and "pax" mean the same thing, peace. Alice had use for the latter amulet on January 27, 1970, when she tried to fend off the psychic attentions of an individual whom she felt was using his psychic powers for evil purposes. Having drawn this amulet she went into deep meditation.

"In trying to transmit peace to him, I found a source of evil was also being transmitted. I was dressed in a white caftan and walking up to the altar to offer myself as an instrument of peace, but I was given the realization that I was not the cause of his troubles. I was told if he would renounce his dealings with the black arts while burning two white candles and profess to assume a new life, the curse would be stopped."

She was told that the sound of pronouncing certain letters of the Hebrew alphabet used in the Kabbalah had a good deal to do with the results. For instance, the letters "p" and "m" sung three times on a descending scale will produce the aura of love. The letter "d," or "daleth," repeated three times and sung in three notes on an ascending scale, will produce the feeling of power or energy. "R" and "v," or "res" and "vau," sung three times with the same intonation, will create the feeling of wisdom while the letters "v" and "j," or "vau" and "jod," also sung three times with the same note, will create an atmosphere of happiness. Knowledge, wisdom, joy, peace, love, power—those seem to be the main desires and the main objectives in magical manipulation. The amulets for each show a curious mixture of Hebrew, Latin, and English words. The writing is both Roman and "celestial" and the symbols are drawn from the Kabbalah, from witchcraft, and from medieval magic.

These amulets are similar in design and purpose to many additional variations used in the so-called "goetic theurgy" or the "key of Solomon"—that is to say, ceremonial magic of the Middle Ages based upon the assumption that there is a huge hierarchy of spirits, demons, and rulers of invisible realms, each with his own symbol or seal.

Arthur Edward Waite has published a large number of these designs in *The Book of Ceremonial Magic*, and it is not my intention to go into them in detail here. But it is amazing to realize that new variations of these amulets come from the hands of Alice McDermott, who is not even familiar with the published ones.

When I questioned her as to the meanings of some of the words found in her drawings, she was quite unable to explain them. The love amulet, for instance, has the words "racel" and "rose" several times on it. The one bringing happiness gives the names of "racel" and "Michael" and I suspect that "racel" and "Raphael" are one and the same since the use of the four archangels is standard practice in both Kabbalah and witch-craft.

*

Why was Alice chosen to transmit this material to the world in cooperation with me? "Be aware of the powers you may possess; alleviate your soul and extend it into the cosmic forces; begin to live," she has written down. And on another occasion she was told, "In finding the way one experiences many trials in accordance with karma and the fulfillment of same. Although karma can be avoided eventually, it does have to be paid. The detachment of karma means the detachment from people, situations, and life in general. One would have to avoid falling into commitments with one another and bonds could not be made."

*

For several days I studied the material Alice had given me on her visit. I decided to probe further into her connection with the Masters and to put her into hypnotic trance to question them directly if possible. The curious mixture of Tibetan magic, Kabbalah, and Dianic paganism, indicated in a preliminary examination of the material Alice had received prior to our recent meeting, seemed to point toward some other goal in these communications.

*

It was on December 5, 1970, that I hypnotized Alice for the first time in connection with her role in these strange communications from Master Nicholas Roerich and his magical teachings. Why was Alice chosen to be the intermediary? I was soon to find out. She went under hypnosis quite easily, and I was able to regress her past her birth. I ordered her to go back in time until she saw another person who might have been herself in a previous lifetime. The belief in reincarnation is an integral part of all witchcraft and magic, and to know Alice's earlier incarnations, if any, would be a valuable key to my understanding of the entire matter.

Finally Alice spoke: "I see myself as a person, a woman. Her name is Aradia. This is Mesopotamia. There is an altar and a ceremony. There are cups, a skull on one side, candles, a bowl, a knife, a mirror, a strange tilted cross made of silver. The building is pyramid-shaped. Now I am outside and there are steps leading up to the top. There are two columns on top and there is fire coming out of them. It is a ceremony, and she is binding herself to someone. She is cutting her wrists and she binds herself to him. They are both in white robes. He wears a crown or something like it and he's of higher rank than she is. She's up there invoking Dionysos; now she falls because she's weak. Someone comes to help her. They put her on a chair. Offerings from the people around are collected—herbs, spices, and eggs—and they are put on the side of the altar."

I watched in fascination. Evidently, Alice had gone back to an entire ceremony in ancient Mesopotamia in which she was either a participant or an observer. I asked that she describe in minute detail what she saw.

"Now there is a black something with water in it and she is looking into it, asking the gods to favor her people, to bless the new crops. There has been a drought and they need water."

Ever the historian, I inquired, "What year are we in?"

"Roerich tells me this is 688 B.C."

The subject seemed to tire, however, and I could not go any further at this session. I quickly returned her to the present and woke her up. She remembered nothing whatever about Mesopotamia or anything she had said under hypnosis. I promised myself to pursue the matter of Aradia on another occasion. Aradia is a prominent witchcraft name. In fact, only a witch would be called Aradia. But the description of the ritual, especially the reference to a person of high rank wearing a crown, left me somewhat puzzled. Later I discovered that Alice had actually described a ritual of Ishtar.

M. E. L. Mallowan in *Man, Myth and Magic* makes reference to a similar festival when he discusses the various aspects of the goddess Ishtar, also called Inanna, the terrifying seductress:

"Inanna-Ishtar presided over one of the most important ceremonies of the year—the ritual marriage of the god, in the course of which the king was wedded to the high priestess and in this way induced for his people the promise of agricultural prosperity."

Two weeks later Alice came to my study to see me. All week long before her arrival I had contemplated making contact with the Master Institute on West 103rd Street.

My idea was to bring Alice to one or both of the Roerich

museums in the hope that something might materialize. Either Roerich himself would make contact or perhaps the atmosphere of Roerich's art might educe some additional material from Alice's own unconscious. I had not discussed this with her.

We first chatted for a few minutes to relax her.

"There is something else I meant to discuss with you, Alice," I finally said, "but I don't want to give you any details at this moment. It has to do with another location which I would like to visit with you."

Alice sat back for a moment as if she were listening to a voice other than either hers or mine. Then she smiled. "Oh, that," she said, "you mean about going to the institute. We won't be able to do that."

I was taken aback. I had not mentioned any institute in her presence, although, unknown to her, I had earlier talked to both institutes. I asked that she clarify her statement. As if she were reading off a prepared report, Alice explained I had intended to take her to an institute connected with Nicholas Roerich, and that we had meant to pick up vibrations in such a place. However, she quickly added, this was not possible; the lady who ran the place was entirely uncooperative and Roerich, she explained, didn't think that it would accomplish anything at all.

In a moment I realized that she was not just reading my mind, but was receiving information from another source. She explained that Roerich did not think much of the display of his art in "the institute," and wouldn't go there to be contacted by us.

I was still confused as to the identity of the lady Nicholas Roerich's spirit did not like.

"What about Mrs. Horch?" I inquired, mentioning the name of the owner of the place on West 103rd Street.

Alice shrugged her shoulders. "He doesn't think that she would *care* about this sort of thing." True, on behalf of Mrs. Horch, her director refused me admission to the Master Insti-

tute in polite but firm terms. She just "didn't care," nor did she
think that the Master had had the slightest interest in the occult!

"And Mrs. Fosdick?" I said casually.

The reaction in Alice was almost violent. "Not her!" she
practically shouted, voicing what she felt was Nicholas Roerich's
view. "Oh no!" It was evident that the Master did not like
Mrs. Fosdick either.

Mrs. Fosdick had thought that Roerich had not been interested in the occult, either; she was polite, and offered to have
us come to the museum, but held out no hope that we could be
alone or that anything psychic might transpire. Under the cir-
cumstances, I realized that neither place was worth a visit.

"Isn't there a place we *can* go and make contact with him?"
I inquired.

Alice emphatically nodded. "Yes, there is. We can go to his
old studio. There is a studio somewhere, I can't get the address,"
she said, still listening to words from beyond. While in New
York in 1921, Nicholas Roerich had stayed at the Hôtel des
Artistes on West 67th Street. It dawned upon me that it might
be the studio.

"Can we get in, though?" I inquired somewhat dubiously.

She nodded. "Yes, we can. I am not sure *how* we will get
in, but we *will*."

Twenty-four hours later I made some telephone calls. The
manager of the Hôtel des Artistes indicated there was no way in
which we could spend a few hours in one of the apartments,
since every apartment was occupied. I then recalled that I had
friends living at this artists' apartment building. I had no idea
whether they would still be there, or whether they would even
be in town, but I took a chance and called Miss Margaret Widdemer, the renowned novelist. Of course, she would be glad to let
us have her apartment for a couple of hours.

The following week we spent our session at the studio of
Margaret Widdemer at the Hôtel des Artistes hoping to pick up

something from the past and Nicholas Roerich's presence in the building. The studio was large and warm, filled with the atmosphere of a creative writer and devoid of the clinical sterility of new buildings. There were several couches and lamps, books on shelves and on tables, and a typewriter with a manuscript page sticking out of it. Miss Widdemer was kind enough to spend a couple of hours across the hall with a neighbor, giving us the privacy of her studio.

As soon as Alice had settled down within the vibrations of the place I began to question her. "Do you feel Roerich present?" I asked. She nodded emphatically. I suggested we start immediately sending her through hypnosis back in time to take up where we had previously left off at my own studio.

Within a matter of minutes, Alice was deeply entranced and had been sent back through her own life until she had once again become a priestess in Mesopotamia. Her face seemed to take on a different expression. There was a sublime glow on it now, a serenity and nobility of purpose different from Alice's ordinary twenty-four-year-old countenance.

*

"What is your name?" I asked.

"Aradia."

"What do you do?"

"I follow the Way. I submit my will. I use my will to obtain others'."

"Do you perform magic?"

"White magic, but there is a knowledge of black."

"Is Roerich one of your teachers?"

"Yes."

"Has he taught you the secrets of Wicca?"

"Yes."

"Have you been anointed a priestess?"

"Yes. By him."

"How many degrees have you earned in Wicca?"

"Three."

"Do you remember the rite of the fire of love, of which you have written under his control?"

"The fire of love. An ointment is used in this. The holy fire is taken and you unite yourself with the fire of man, the fire, the Masters; and you use the fire as a symbol."

"How many take part in it?"

"In this group there should be eleven; six men and five women. Roerich is the priest."

"Who is the priestess?"

"I was at that time. I was being united with him, through fire."

"What was your name then?"

"Aradia."

"Describe the ceremony."

"It was the mingling of the blood and the soul; the cutting of the wrists and the mingling of the blood, and the astral flight of the soul; and the taking of an herb potion to relieve the pain from the cutting."

"What is in the potion?"

"Leaves from a certain plant to make a poultice, a plant with pricks on the end of it, and long, skinny leaves. You also take the juice internally."

"How did the ceremony proceed from there?"

"You're united with him. The others make a circle around you; there is salt sprinkled around. Your hands are taken, and where you were cut they are put together, and they are bound. Your souls hover over, and they unite together. After this you drink of the wine, and then a candle is burned; within the sacred fire you dispose of the herbs that you have used. As soon as the herbs are burned, the fire is placed in the middle of the circle, and the wine is used to extinguish the fire. Then the salt is placed within the circle, and the remainders of this are buried."

"What follows this?"

"After this, another ceremony follows it. The ceremony

where you and your mate are united, in front of the high priest. You come before the high priest just to ask his blessing, that you will have a fertile marriage together; and he blesses you, and he puts salt on both your tongues. Then you give him bands of silver."

"What do you do with these bands of silver?"

"You wear them on your fingers."

"How are you dressed?"

"In white robes again, but trimmed in silver. After that there is still another ceremony. The ceremony of Getumah. You are given a gemstone, which you use to protect yourself and to obtain power. You hold the gemstone in the palm of your hand, and your hand is raised upward, and when you ask for energy, the gemstone will purify the energy you receive. This gemstone must be purified in a potion of herbs before you can use it."

"Is the ceremony of the rings a marriage ceremony, or is it a ceremony of union between men and women as such?"

"A ceremony of union between men and women."

"Not necessarily a marriage ceremony?"

"No."

"When is the union consummated?"

"When they reach the third degree."

"Describe this."

"The third degree is taken. The man and woman are brought forth together and they are bound on their hands and then the feet. And then their hands are bound together in front of one another. Flowers are placed on the woman's head, a wreath of flowers; and a wreath of leaves is placed on the man's head. The medals they wear are exchanged, and he becomes her counterpart as she becomes his. Usually these two people are married to one another."

"Are all of them married one to another?"

"In this particular group, yes. Except for Roerich; he is not married to anyone in this group; his wife is not present."

"Whom does he unite with?"

"He unites with the high priestess."

"Who is the high priestess?"

"I am in this group."

"After the hands are bound, what follows?"

"After the hands are bound in this ceremony of the third degree, there is a blessing with salt water, there is chanting by the people, and drums and brass."

"How many participants are there?"

"Eleven, all dressed in white, with different-colored trims on the robes."

"What is the next step?"

"They are given a sip of wine. Then they are asked if they *want* to be one. They answer yes. Then they are asked, do they abide within the law, and they answer yes; then they are asked, does the law abide within them, and they answer yes. Will they do the best they can to preserve the rights of the law. They answer yes. Are they sincere, and they answer yes. They are asked if they have been one before, so that the degrees of initiation will remain one together, and they answer yes."

"When the questions have all been answered, what follows?"

"Then the hands are bound again with another rope with three knots in it. Then the rope is taken off, and is untied, and *two knots* remain at the end. The rope then goes around the waist of the woman, and another one goes around the waist of the man. A potion is given to both of them. If it tastes bitter, they're insincere. They don't know this at the time when they are asked how does it taste."

"And if it tastes sweet?"

"Then they are telling the truth."

"How are they rewarded?"

"They are accepted to the third degree. Then they are given their instruments, and a book. Knives with handles of copper, brass, and silver and a gemstone which belongs to them, and a book on the writings of the degrees of initiation."

"Do they stay on, or are they led elsewhere?"

"They stay on together to meditate. Then they go right to the back room of the temple, for instruction. When they know the ways, when they control the elementals, then the union takes place. One cannot go without the other; they must both be ready and prepared."

"When they are ready and prepared, does the union take place at any special time or place?"

"It takes place on the eve before a great holiday."

"Which holiday?"

"Sometime in May, the virgins' holiday. All the young children, dressed in white, bring flowers to their virgin, and oils."

"Who is the virgin?"

"One of the goddesses, Diana."

"Is it on this holiday that the union of the couple is celebrated?"

"Yes, only within the group. After the union has been completed, they celebrate because now they are *high*, and they show that they have mastered the control. The hardest element to master is fire; the easiest to master is the air, and the water."

"In which way are they *high*?"

"Their spiritual souls are higher."

"Is this because of the union?"

"Yes. The two have come together and *exchanged energy*."

"Do they do this in the middle of the group?"

"Yes."

"What does the group do during that time?"

"They meditate, to give them more energy to bring up higher vibrations."

"Is it through their *union* that new energy is created?"

"Yes."

"When mastering magic the Tibetan way, after the third degree, what follows?"

"Then complete unity with the Masters. The Masters teach you themselves, and you become part of their force."

"Losing your individuality?"

"No; you never lose your individuality, you work upon your individuality."

"Can this magic change the natural law?"

"Within limitations, yes, it does. There is Euphrates, which will take the place of earth. Every time disaster threatens the earth, all those of the third degree and above shall be transported by magic means to this planet, and saved."

"Where is Euphrates?"

"In position to take the earth's place."

"Has the Master, Roerich, determined to communicate with me through you, to give the world some knowledge it does not now possess?"

"Yes; the knowledge of the degrees after the third degree, the way of the lama, the way to communicate with the Masters. But it has to be brought down to the level where all can understand it."

"How is it brought down?"

"Through you. You will find a way."

"Is this *magic* of sorts that I am to tell the world about?"

"Yes; those who read it will interpret it *as such*. Others who are not meant to see will just read the *words*, and they will be empty to them. There are five planes of existence on which to work. The mind is one; the heart another. You will reach people this way."

I looked around the semidark studio thoughtfully.

"Does Roerich tell you when he lived here?" I asked.

"He says he lived here a very short time. Just to do some paintings. He didn't like the United States that much; he preferred the oriental way of life."

That, of course, was true, but unknown to Alice.

"Coming back here, does he remember things?"

"He *wanted* to come back here. He attaches himself to my

body to use it at times—to feel, to touch things, to see how they are; not having a body in his state as a Master. At this time he is not permitted to use a body on earth in the United States. He has a body that he can use through Morea, in Tibet. Morea is a Master who lives in Tibet."

"Does he still consider you a priestess in this incarnation?"

"Yes; but I'm not ready to instruct yet. I have much to read and much to learn all over again."

A short time later I brought Alice out of the trance. As before, she remembered absolutely nothing of what had come through her lips while in the hypnotic state. We went to thank Miss Widdemer for her hospitality and after a few minutes left what was once the studio building of the late, but very much alive, Nicholas Roerich.

*

On December 18, 1970, Alice came to my study again for another trance session. By now I was well aware of the fact that the source of information for much of the material lay in two directions. Firstly, Alice's own reincarnation memories as a high priestess of ancient witchcraft in Mesopotamia, and possibly additional reincarnation material also involving witchcraft which might yet come to the surface as we worked along. Secondly, Alice's own personality as a medium evidently derived information from her mentor and control Nicholas Roerich. While she was unable to recall anything about previous incarnations in the conscious state, she was, of course, well aware of Roerich's presence even while not entranced. In trance, however, both the reincarnation material and Roerich's instructions came through much clearer.

I had studied the magical material and incantations Alice had received prior to our working together. While I was satisfied that they could not have originated with her, even under the influence of her study with the yoga group, there was much in the spells themselves that needed clarification and explanation.

"I would like to ask you and your guides," I said, "to comment on the meaning of the following spell: 'This man is mine; I draw the powers of the sea and air; the flame is mine. I send thee strength of almighty God. I am one with him; klim hum. Long time short time all time is mine. I strip thee of thy foulness. Be thou mine. Open and I shall seek the good.' What is the purpose of this spell?"

"Purification, by the high priestess, to purify a person you've already made contact with, and to keep him *yours*. The *klim hum* sets up good vibrations—your love, kindness, desire."

"Does this ritual take place under certain conditions?"

"There is blessing of salt water and burning of a white candle, and the recitation of the words."

"If this is magic, does it keep the person tied to the one who uses the ritual?"

"Yes, but not necessarily against their will."

"What does *klim hum* mean?"

"The intonation of certain vowels produces effects. These are dedicated to the elements: ha, ra, va, ba, ya. They're dedicated to air, water, the elements in general, strength, power, knowledge, so as to draw upon them."

"Can magic overcome barriers?"

"It can, depending upon the person's karma. What is meant to be for that person can be removed at times, or its impart lessened, to an extent."

"If an individual has a desire to contact another person through magic, will the power reach the other person regardless of whether that person is attuned to the sender or not?"

"Yes, it will."

"Will the receiver be conscious of it?"

"Yes, but it depends on the relationship between receiver and sender. If there is a close rapport between them, then the receiver will know from whom the message is, but if there is no rapport between them, then the receiver will not be aware of what he is doing or why he is doing it."

"Is a spell something that must be *allowed* to happen because it is karmically prescribed?"

"If it is karmically prescribed, it will happen; but the time can be changed for the happening, and with adepts it will happen in a lesser degree. For example, he says to me, there was a pupil of his who had to do certain work, but it was necessary that he have a burn. Well, his hand was burned, and at the same time his hand was healed, so that he could go on and finish his work."

"Must some acts be performed in order to get on with the relationship, or the future?"

"Yes."

"Are the Masters, like Roerich, directing these relationships?"

"They do."

"What is the ultimate goal?"

"To help mankind attain the higher self! There is much work to be done in this world, but there are other worlds, other places that have to be worked upon. Their ultimate goal is to attain pure energy."

"In the performance of magic ritual by individuals, is their working together creating something larger than what they themselves have put into it?"

"Definitely. They are only instruments being used in the working force of magic."

"When the priestess performs a magic ritual, who works through her?"

"The goddess Diana."

"What is Diana's law?"

"The law of love of mankind; complete self-fulfillment within the rites."

"For each and every member of mankind?"

"For the chosen members, the adepts."

"What is her prescription for her favored ones?"

"You must have perfect love for one another. Sincerity in what you are doing. There are certain things that must be

taken from other ways, other religions, that of Tibet; that of
the Druids; the Rosicrucians; the Masons—they all must be
studied because they have much truth within them."

"Do these laws transcend or nullify the conventional law and
moral attitudes of our society?"

"Yes. But why must we be conventional? Magic is different."

*

In an earlier trance session Alice had described a recurrent
dream vision in what she assumed to be a cave in Tibet. She
described her mystic initiation into that group of white-robed
worshipers who had worked directly with the Masters. I had
already begun to realize that all mystic initiations, all forms of
pagan religions, have certain things in common. There are
parallels, there are similarities of approach, yet there are differences of ritual style and, of course, texts. Today Alice was speaking of the worship of Diana, that is to say, the witchcraft of
ancient Greece and the Western world including Great Britain.
This had been brought to the British Isles in pre-Hellenic times
by the people of ancient Greece who preceded the classical
Greeks.

Although Diana is known by many names, it is always the
same moon goddess that is being worshiped. If Alice had any
knowledge of the Dianic initiation in the trance state, that
knowledge must come from an external source, I argued, and
I wanted to test the extent of her knowledge.

*

"Alice," I said, "can you describe the ritual of the Dianic
initiation?"

"The high priest and high priestess are present, and only the
one who is to be initiated. She or he is brought forth before
them, and initiated into the coven according to the rules of
Diana. He or she is asked if he wants to join. Will he be
faithful to them? Is he sincere? He must answer all these questions correctly. Prayers are being recited over his head from a

book. Afterward, there are more prayers and a blessing of instruments, the knives, the cords; and after that he is bound, the hands, the feet. The high priestess initiates him, and if it were a female the high priest would initiate her. They're on their knees, and they have relations, but it is all spiritual, because sex produces the highest vibrations, the highest psychic vibrations that can be created. Then these vibrations are passed on to the others in the coven. In the ways of Tibet the initiation is different, more on the side of spirit than on physical contact, though when you have reached the stage of the Masters, it may be both."

"When have you been taught the ways of Diana?"

"Long time ago. I have worshiped her in many lifetimes. In Mesopotamia I was a high priestess, and a magician."

"Before your present incarnation, do you recall another life?"

*

After a moment Alice had retraced her steps into England, where she lived under the name Joan Burlington. It was an unpleasant experience. She had died by falling off a horse while only in her twenties. She remembered well the farmhouse in which she lived but wasn't sure whether it was in Suffolk or Esssex. She was a member of a witch coven and they would practice in a field within a circle of old stones where an abbey once stood, and they always met on the new moon and on the full moon. The coven comprised eleven people, though at times there were only seven. She remembered vividly why she died so young. There was a man named Charles Bottomworth who was after her because he had wanted her to marry him and she had preferred John Burlington. In revenge, Charles was going to tell her husband that she was a witch. This she did not want to happen, so she raced home trying to head him off, but the horse stumbled and she fell to her death.

She had trouble remembering the details of her life in England and the coven of which she was a member because it wasn't a good coven, she explained; there were some bad vibrations in it. I asked her to tell me of the rituals they performed.

"It was mostly farmers; they wanted good crops, and it was to bless their crops. It was when the moon was full in the sky, usually about twelve to three o'clock in the morning. We left home and assembled in the fields. We greeted one another: we said, 'Blessed be.' We just talked for a few minutes, then we would make a circle, there was a high priest, and we would *come together*, and then he would bless the crops."

"How were you attired?"

"Without clothes."

"Were you anointed?"

"Yes, with balm, which had herbs in it, rosemary and others. It was supposed to make us more holy, and hold in our psychic energy."

"Did it work?"

"Yes."

"Did you sing or dance?"

"Yes, to raise power."

"Do you remember any spells?"

"Grow, crops, grow; make the crops grow. High, low, tall, short, all the crops will grow. Wheat fields, barley fields, corn fields, grow."

"Did you appeal to any particular god or goddess?"

"To Diana."

"What did the priest represent?"

"Thor."

"Did he have any symbols of office?"

"He had horns."

"How many men and women were there in your group?"

"Sometimes three women, four men; sometimes five women, six men."

"Did you work with the priest?"

"Sometimes. I don't remember—there was much hate."

"Was it the priest's fault?"

"Yes, because he only wanted to learn satanic rites."

"How did they differ from the ones you liked?"

"Sacrificing of animals, shedding of blood. Just sex for sex's sake. Doing evil to others for no reason. Greed, and money. All he was interested in was to attain wealth, to keep himself young. And these are not the ways of Diana."

"Did you leave this group?"

"Yes; I practiced by myself. An angel would come. Racel. The Masters sent him."

"What did you do in the angel's presence?"

"Make a magic circle, and read from the book the angel had brought."

"How did the ritual differ from the one that you had known?"

"It was completely in Hebrew. I didn't understand it, but I was told to do it, so I did it."

"What were some of the things you did?"

"I learned to control power, the elements, and to help the farmers, and I tried to destroy Charles, the high priest, for the evil he was doing."

"And did you?"

"Almost. I died before I had a chance to finish."

"What rite did you perform?"

"The angel was to be sent to him. I had to read from the book of the angels, a very special book that had to be kept in the house for a year, and it would bless the house. The angel would remain at all times in the circle, and I would work with him, obtaining energy from him. My hands would be crossed within the circle, and two rays would come down, and I would obtain psychic energy. I would battle psychically with Charles."

"When you were killed in the accident, where did you go?"

"I was with the Masters for a while; then I was told I must be reborn again to finish my work. I had much karma that I had created, and I must fulfill my karma."

"Did they tell you when and where you would be reborn?"

"No."

"Where did you find yourself next?"

"Here, in my present incarnation."

"Do you consider yourself still a priestess, with a mission to fulfill?"

"Yes, there is much more to learn. Tibet, Diana, the Masters—they must be combined. Diana is the first stage, Tibet the second, and the Masters are the final stage."

"Which is the next major pagan holiday?" I asked, testing her knowledge of the Old Religion further.

"Candlemas."

"What is being celebrated then?"

"The changing of the seasons."

"How is the Candlemas ritual performed?"

"Through the union of the high priest and priestess. That is the blessing. There is also a Tibetan holiday at the same time. He's telling me they should be combined."

"What power is gained?"

"Your magical power is heightened, and knowledge is brought forth to you. When the moon is high in the sky, that should be the most powerful hour."

*

Since the Master had suggested a Tibetan ceremony and held out the possibility of gaining unusual powers from it, I felt it was at least worth a try. But where do you find a Tibetan holy ground in Manhattan? As if I had been directed, my eye fell upon a listing in the New York telephone directory, "Office of Tibet." I quickly discovered that there was no Tibetan monastery or sanctuary within New York City.

The few Tibetans who lived in and around the metropolitan area worshiped the ancient gods of Tibet at a monastery located in the community of Freewood Acres near Farmingdale, New Jersey. A few more telephone calls and a brief discussion with the Reverend Yishi Tsedu and permission was granted

for Alice McDermott and me to visit the lamasery. I was given
exact directions on how to get there, but when we set out on a
snowy afternoon, we had trouble finding the right route. Perhaps we should have waited until Candlemas, which comes in
February, to attempt this, but I was impatient. I therefore
chose an earlier holiday, Yule, to visit the Tibetan shrine.
True, Yule is not one of the major holidays of the pagan
calendar, but it would be interesting to see whether anything
special happened to Alice when she was entranced in such an
exotic place as a Tibetan lamasery. We arrived about two hours
late. The kind monks received us nevertheless with true Eastern
hospitality.

The lamasery itself is a simple wooden structure and belies
its splendor when seen from the outside. We almost entered
a Russian Orthodox Church next door by mistake until we
realized we were in the wrong pew. The monks readily permitted us to go to the temple itself, a large hall at one end of which
there was an altar adorned with flowers, Buddhas, and offerings.
There they suggested we meditate by ourselves, but Alice felt
out of place in so large a hall. Instead I requested permission
to meditate in a small anteroom next to the temple itself.

We were given some oriental tea, which was very welcome as
the night was terribly cold and we had not had dinner. Then
I put Alice into a hypnotic trance to see if anything unusual
might come through to her on this occasion. Unfortunately,
Alice had not been feeling well that afternoon. The Master
manifested as soon as she was in trance, but all the power
generated was needed to heal her. Then an offering was made
in the name of Diana and also to the Buddha of Tibet. We
could not stay any longer. As we left I felt as if I had myself
received a healing.

*

We interrupted our work during the Christmas season, but
during that time Alice received information from her mentor
concerning an initiation ritual. First, there was a special incan-

tation to be spoken during the anointing of the body with consecrated oil prior to the initiation:

"Omen hetar! Omen hetar, I am thee and thou art mine. I have nothing which is not thine. In thy name, Aradia, behold thy servant. I am thee and thou art me. We are one for all eternity."

Here are the details of the "robed initiation":

Challenger: "Whence come you?"

Candidate: "From the North, a place of great darkness."

Challenger: "Where do you go?"

Candidate: "I travel East in search of light."

Challenger: "What passwords dost thou bring?"

Candidate: "Perfect love and perfect trust."

Challenger: "I, the guardian of the watchtower of the North, forbid thee entrance. Thou canst not enter the holy place from the North save thou first be purified and consecrated. Who vouches for you?"

Summoner: "I, guide of souls, do so."

Challenger: "Child of darkness, approach thou the watchtower of the North and receive of me the bonds of death and blessing of earth."

Evidently, the ritual is not complete, but this is all Alice got on that occasion in private meditation at home.

*

A little later that evening she was given what appears to be her own oath of acceptance for an initiation ceremony. It is interesting to note how similar it is to other forms used in the secret initiations, and yet there are also significant differences which are certainly not the work of Alice in her conscious state.

"I (Candidate's witchcraft name), in the presence of all here assembled, man or god, living or dead, do of my free will most solemnly swear that I shall ever keep secret those things entrusted to my ears alone by the coven, except it be to a proper person, properly prepared within such circle as I am now in; and that I shall never deny the secrets to such a person should he be properly vouched for by a fellow member of the coven. All this I swear upon my life, now and hereafter, and may those powers I possess, now or hereafter, turn against me should I break this most solemn oath! So mote it be."

"Mote," meaning "let," is a rare word used in magic. I doubt very much that Alice would be familiar with such a term in her everyday life. When I questioned her about it, she had no knowledge of it.

*

Also during the same meditation period Alice was given a prescription for Sabbath incense: bay, laurel, vervain, wormwood, fig leaves, and fir branches. A sabbath oil should be made from wild parsley root, celery root, poplar leaves, saffron, cinquefoil, and it should be purified in vegetable oil during the waxing of the moon, or in pure alcohol and later mixed with oil. The communicator, presumably Nicholas Roerich, ended his "transmission" to Alice with the reminder, "The witches' wheel is the way—find the witches' wheel!" The witches' wheel, of course, is the calendar. What he meant was that all pagan ceremony must be in rigid accord with the natural movement of the earth in relation to nature. The calendar, as Fred Adams has pointed out, is the backbone of proper living.

*

On January 10, 1971, I had another lengthy trance session with Alice, at which I took up the matter of the Sabbath oil again. She explained that it was one of three basic oils that may be used on high holidays. "Where is this put?" I asked. "On the glands of your body. Your body is anointed with the oil." Earlier she had also mentioned the use of "musk" in certain rituals. I asked what musk was. "Musk is cosmic dust. It falls to earth and is eaten by goats and then regained from the testicles after the goats die. Tibetan villagers collect it and it is considered a precious substance. Musk restores the cosmic energy within the body. It can prevent cancer if taken every day, and tiny amounts are sufficient."

*

I decided to ask the Masters to enlarge upon my storehouse of knowledge of spells and incantations. The intermingling of three different strains of religious backgrounds was unique and quite possibly the result might be more powerful than the incantations of, let us say, Celtic Wicca alone or Tibetan mysticism alone or the Kabbalah alone. Here we had all three together for the first time. All this, of course, was seen and formulated through the eyes and mind of Nicholas Roerich and channeled to me, for the world to know, through the mediumship of Alice McDermott.

It was really immaterial whether she knew these secrets in a previous incarnation or unconsciously in her present one. If these spells and incantations work at all, they would work beyond the boundaries of time and space.

*

"Without disturbing the natural course of karma," Alice explained, "there is one word to prevent accidents from happening and to change some destiny. It can never be used by a person for himself, only for others. The word is *raja*. Of Tibetan origin, it is the evocation of all deities, will change an event from happening, will stop an accident, will prevent something dreadful."

"Is there an incantation if you *want* certain events to take place?"

"You invoke the elements: Fire of light, fire of love—send forth thy power, assist me and guide me, that my will may be one with the Masters. Then call upon an angel: I bid you to come unto me, Michael, Gabriel, and Racel, I bid you to come unto me, assist me that my will may be done. I bid you to do my will, that my will be done."

"Do you have to specify what it is that you want done?"

"Yes. You have to tell them."

"Can you use your own words for that?"

"You can, because they come to you in a circle."

"How many have to be present to do this?"

"Only you. You can do it by yourself."

"Do you have to perform any ritual at the same time?"

"You have to make a circle for them. You have to be blessed. You have to be purified. No food, no water, for twenty-four hours before. Your soul must be exorcised of all evil doings and temptations, because this can be used either as black or white, depending upon who you beckon to come. Gabriel, Racel, and Michael are white forces."

"Who are the black forces?

"You call upon the children of Satan; you call upon Beelzebub, you call upon an "angel of light," but it will not be an angel of *light*."

"Are these angels real entities, or are they symbols?"

"Entities. They exist all around us."

"Were they at one time human beings?"

"Yes. They were created by the Masters, to do their bidding. To assist in the program of the world."

"How long ago was this done?"

"For our world, it cannot be measured in time. It was a long time ago, in man's words. For us, forever will end; for them, forever will never end."

"Are these the same 'angels' mentioned in Christian theology?"

"Yes."

"Would you give me the formula for a love spell, when one person wishes to implant a feeling of love in another?"

" 'Fire of light, fire of love, bring forth the one I want tonight. Fire of light, fire of love, bring forth unto me.' It must be said three times. He will come to you. There must be burning of red candles and orange candles. Three candles are needed, two red and one orange, or three red."

"Is there any ritual that must be performed?"

"No, but afterward you must impose upon him that you are one with him, by saying we are one, we are one, over and over again, after you have recited the incantation, before he comes."

"Will that person come to you?"

"Within twenty-four hours—well, within a *reasonable* time; it depends where the person is located.

"What must the one who has done the spell do next?"

"Eventually you have to renew it; if you don't wish to renew it or break relationships, you don't. But you have to renew it on the new moon, every month."

"Is there anything needed other than the candles and the spell?"

"Some people use flowers put in front of the picture of the person summoned."

"To prepare yourself to cast a spell, do you have to do anything yourself?"

"You have to be purified, physically, so you don't have any elements that would work against you, by anointing yourself with oil and taking musk."

"The oil used for purification, what is it made of?"

"Regular kitchen oil, with a bit of rosemary, a little musk, nutmeg, thyme, cumin—just normal spices you would have in the house. You say your name, 'I anoint myself, with this oil, to make my will one with the Masters, that I may do their bidding and that my bidding may be done.' "

"Do you cover your entire body with that?"

"Yes. Very thinly, a very fine coat. The spell works best during the new moon, or on a Wednesday. Wednesdays are good for casting spells, I am told."

"What about a spell for good health?"

"First there is an herbal mixture to be taken. It depends on what's wrong with the person. Then you say: 'Good health, bad health, go away, bad health, come again unto me the good health that I need, stay with me, make me strong, that I may give it unto someone else. Good health, bad health, right or wrong, give to me this good health which will make me strong.' "

"Is there anything you must do while you say these words?"

"You're placing the herbs in an aluminum or copper pan, any kind which is clean, *not* for cooking. You add water and boil them, and after you've taken them, you take the remaining herbs and bury them in the ground, because they have taken the evil away from the person."

"Does the person have to be present?"

"No."

"Can you use this for yourself, if you are not well?"

"No."

*

When Alice came back to my study on January 22 for another trance session, she brought with her the drawing of an amulet she had received a few days before. Prominent in the drawing was a pentagram, a moon crescent, and several smaller "seals" of protective deities. At the same time, she was given another drawing in meditation, a number of single letters and a pentagram flanking three interlinked triangles in the center. This drawing was the only one of all her drawings not in the form of an amulet. Alice could throw no light on the meaning of these drawings; however, on top of the sheet she had written a protective spell:

"By water and fire I conjure thee that they remain within thy frame. No adverse thought nor entity. Hear my will, attend to me, as my word, so mote it be!"

Again Alice went into deep trance rather quickly since by now it was a matter of routine to get her under. This time I decided to probe more deeply into the existence and nature of the Masters.

*

"Tell me," I began, "*where* do the Masters exist?"

"They exist on several planes, depending upon what degree of wisdom, or essence, they have reached.

"Were they people like you and me before?"

"Some of them, yes. Some of them not."

"Who makes them into Masters?"

"By fulfillment of the karmic law, the eternal forces join and bid the soul to beckon forth. They are raised to a level, and then to the next, and by fullfillment they are raised to each level, until they reach the degree of Master."

"What is the ultimate goal?"

"You cannot define the ultimate goals. They are incomprehensible to man; they are part of energy, they are *being*; they are fulfillment of the higher self; they are that being which men call *God*."

"And what is God?"

"God is love; God is everything."

"Is there a person, as we understand the term?"

"There is the combination of all these into that one being. There is *one higher force*."

"Is God a person?"

"God is not a person. God is pure energy; God is pure existence; God is, God will be."

"How did God come into being?"

"He is eternity. He is the essence which man cannot understand."

"Why cannot man understand him?"

"To us there is no end to an eternity; to God there is an end to an eternity, because eternity upon eternity upon eternity there is God."

"Was there ever a time when there was no God?"

"Never."

"Does God fill all the universe, or only that which concerns itself with the earth?"

"God fills everything."

"If God is not an individual but a force, how did the force grow? Was it always at the same strength, or was it at any time smaller?"

"It was always of the same strength, but to fulfill the lower parts of creation in a complex system, it was necessary to enlarge upon this force. Therefore, the creation of the Masters."

"Who made these rules?"

"There is the unwritten law, the *Elohim*. The Elohim is God."

"Has God a functioning mind?"

"As it can be described by man, there is a functioning side of God, yes. There are many faces and many sides, because you cannot limit nor describe something to man which is beyond his capacity of understanding."

*

This was pretty strong stuff to swallow for someone as scientifically orientated and trained as I am. Of course, it made sense, philosophically speaking. I have always run up against a kind of wall when I have tried to approach a rational definition of the deity. But if I were to accept these instructions and the very fact that there are Masters on the other side of life, I still felt the need of some reinforcement, rationally speaking, something that would perhaps only in a small and indirect way assure me that there was indeed a chain of command, or communication, if you prefer. Everything that had happened so far with Alice was astonishing, and there was no doubt in my mind whatsoever that much of the material, if not all of it, coming through her was beyond her own capacities as an individual.

Still, one might argue that theoretically the material and information could be obtained at least in part through exhaustive research by someone well trained in the occult sciences. Clearly what I needed was something that could not have been researched by anyone, no matter how clever.

I was yet to be given that proof. Prior to my departure for California, I had arranged for a meeting with Alice on February 1, 1971. This was to be an attempt to elicit additional details concerning the Candlemas ritual on the very day of the festival in the hope that the actual date would prove to be a stimulant to her memory or open the channels of communication wider than on any other day without such significance. I had always been aware of the need to coordinate the calendar with my quest. As usual, I had put Alice into trance and she proceeded to speak the proper Candlemas ritual. Suddenly she halted and shook her head, informing me that she could not complete the ritual at that time. Another person had to be brought into the picture before the ritual could be properly concluded, she explained. It was for me to meet this individual and go through an initiation with him, learning some important facts and sharpening my psychic and physical senses. Somewhat surprised, I asked who that individual was. Without hesitation she gave me the name of the man I was to find. It was a witchcraft name I had never heard before.

Because of the oath of secrecy in the pagan religions I cannot give this name here in print, except to say that it was the name of an obscure hero in Greek mythology, known for his great flights of imagination. "You will find D. in California," Alice said. She knew of my impending California trip so that was hardly a revelation.

I dismissed the matter and left the following day for California. Two days later, on February 4, I found myself at the headquarters of the O.T.A., the Order of the Temple of Astarte, in Pasadena. I had just been through a specific ritual and now the social hour had brought together old friends. Among them was Fred Adams, of whom I have spoken earlier in this book. We chatted amiably for a few moments, and then Fred out of a clear sky informed me that he had decided to change his witchcraft name from the one he had borne for many years. "My new name is D.," he said lightly, and a cold shiver ran up and down my back. It was the same obscure mythological figure Alice had named on February 1, *three days before*. "When did you decide to do this?" I asked Fred. "Last night," he replied, and looked at me quizzically. I then told him why I had asked about the time, and he, too, took this to be proof positive of the wonderous workings of the Masters.

As a result of my own further initiation into Feraferia, I returned to New York with greater knowledge and an additional sense of advancement. It was after that period that so much more evidential material came through Alice's mediumship.

The end is not yet in sight, but the beginning alone is very promising. There was no way in which Alice could have known of Fred's decision to change his pagan name to D., nor can this be explained as long-distance telepathy since Fred had not thought of it until after Alice had informed me.

*

During the subsequent weeks we met again and again, retracing our steps and rounding out the material Nicholas Roerich wanted Alice to transmit to me. On several occasions he informed us that he preferred to be called Nicole rather than Nicholas. By now we were on friendly terms.

At the end of February I felt that the time had come to put some basic questions about paganism to the Masters. In a way, this would round out their messages to me and through me to the world, and put into simple and precise language what in their view the pagan movement stood for.

Through the entranced Alice, I asked first of all what in their opinion constituted a pagan?

"A pagan is one who worships the natural law, who sees a god in everything."

"How does a pagan treat people who differ with him, religiously or politically?"

"As his equal. With love."

"How does a pagan feel about war and violence?"

"He dislikes it, does not want to have any part of it."

"How does a pagan view the future of this country?"

"The United States? Too militaristic. Too much pressure upon the young."

"What is the pagan way in marriage, love, and sex relations?"

"To be free and united together with the one you love."

"Does the pagan believe in the traditional institution of marriage?"

"No."

"Does the pagan feel that individuals should be free to relate to others as their emotions guide them?"

"Yes, to relate to each situation, as their emotions guide them to do what is right, as long as it does not *hurt anyone else*."

"What are the basic freedoms of the pagan way?"

"Freedom to give justice to the divine force. Freedom of self, and the spirit to unite. Freedom to be with others, to live in accordance with one's own beliefs."

"What deity do you feel will be the most powerful deity worshiped as the years go by?"

"Diana will be."

"What will a typical worship of Diana be like in the future?"

"There will be a gathering of people, and they will sing and dance together, and have their circle, and they will have their energy force."

"How many people will come together?"

"Between seven and thirteen."

"Will they meet in special places?"

"Yes; indoors or outdoors, depending on the climate. The ceremony begins with the drawing of the circle large enough to have the whole group enter into it. In most cases it will be the priestess who will draw the circle. There will be many things that will be changed in the old ways of Diana, in the ways that are traditional now. Women will become more prevalent. They will become more adept, they will know more about the religion, the way. Next there will be symbols placed in the corners, to the four winds. The circle will be blessed, and purified with salt and water. If someone in the coven needs something, it is made known *beforehand*, so that they can prepare for it."

"And what is done to make these wishes come true?"

"The group force works together, and they ask the goddess to invoke her power upon them, so that they may fulfill their tasks in her name."

"After that, what do they do?"

"The high priestess and priest come together to join forces. The group may also. And it is the *psychic* energy that they receive. They recharge their own powers, and they may use it to fulfill their own desires."

"Does this always work?"

"Yes."

"Do they have to have their wishes strictly defined before they start the ceremony?"

"Yes."

"When this energy is released, will they have new strength because of it, or will they be depleted of power?"

"At times they are given new strength because of it."

"Are there any special preparations these people will go through in future meetings in honor of Diana?"

"They must be bathed in salt water immediately before it."

"Will all members of the group do this at the same time?"

"No, one by one. The high priestess begins."

"When all of them have partaken of the salt water, what do they do next?"

"They form their circle. Then there is the anointing of the body, to bring out the psychic energies within you; to open up the organs of the body, the glands. Each person usually anoints himself before they enter the circle. They will join forces in various ways. One group will sing and dance and fall down after they are tired, and they will feel energy released from them. Other groups will have intercourse and feel energy released from them in that manner."

"Which is the *highest* form of 'power raising'?"

"The joining together of two forces. It is not that of passion or lust or desire, but mainly of fulfilling a purpose upon a goal: to raise energy."

"In future days, will this be the way of the pagans?"

"Yes."

"Will this be generally accepted?"

"Yes."

"Do you foresee any difficulties this may cause in the present structure of society and morality?"

"Definitely. But the generations are changing, and the older generations will just have to accept it."

*

For the present the Masters had instructed Alice and, through her, me, and through me, the public to the extent they had evidently intended to. If some of the instructions seemed revolutionary, one must only realize that there is no *compulsion* to accept them or carry them out.

Paganism is not one big orgy. Neither is it an intellectual, spiritual withdrawal from the world for the purpose of denying the body, and elevating the spirit. The magic of the Masters is really nothing more than a more perfect way of combining man's inherent forces on all three levels—physical, mental, and spiritual. If in our present society and at this time we have not yet freed our physical unfoldment from its shackles, then these recommendations must indeed sound revolutionary and to some, even immoral. But they are honest and natural ways of living and nothing that is in tune with nature can ever be wrong. At least not from a transcendental, higher point of view.

It may well be that in the future the teachings of Nicholas Roerich and the Masters through the channel of Alice McDermott and others will become formalized in such a way that there will be schools and training centers where people can go to be instructed or to discuss and learn that which is of interest to them.

If I have been chosen by these sources to be their spokesman for the present, I have done so without any attempt at influencing their judgment, and have done my best to be as accurate as humanly possible in reporting what they have to say. No doubt they will say other things on other occasions yet to come.

AFTERWORD

THE PAGAN MANIFESTO

Are the new pagans merely a far-out movement among jaded sophisticated human adventurers who have seen and heard a lot and are now looking for new frontiers? I don't think so. The pagan revival movement must have its fair share of undesirables, of disturbed individuals, of those who are entering it for the wrong reasons. Every new movement, religious or mundane, has some unwanted people in it. Eventually, such individuals fall by the wayside by the sheer weight of their ignorance and false orientation. The overwhelming majority of those who profess to be pagans today earnestly seek a different path toward the Deity and are not motivated by destructive or unhealthy forces.

As yet it is not fully respectable to proclaim one's paganism to the world if one holds high office or a social position which one values. On the other hand, there is nothing in the pagan cults I have seen that requires one to denounce the Christian faith or any other faith for that matter. To the contrary, neo-paganism suggests that one live up to the *original* concept of one's orthodox faith, for if both beliefs are examined it will be found that in their basic forms most orthodoxies contain religious concepts and commands also championed by paganism.

Pagans are pantheists. They see God everywhere and everything contains God. They have no quarrel with other religions and cheerfully accept the gods of others among theirs.

Paganism is on the march because it offers worshipers something the Christian and other orthodox religions cannot offer. It is the only philosophy of religion combining spiritual and physical oneness with the Deity in small personal gatherings without obligation or dogmatic threat and in a way that stimulates interest rather than creating a sense of routine and coercion. Christianity and the other world religions could have done the same thing. Their God could have been representative of nature just as the deity of paganism is. Self-fulfillment is nondenominational, but, for reasons of politics and state, the churches demanded an alienation from the forces of nature, perhaps with the misguided notion that denial of nature would enhance the spirit.

The new pagans know very well that nature and spirit go hand in hand, one feeding the other, one starving without the other. So the cycle is complete. In speaking of magic and of Tibet and the East I have ultimately found my way back to Diana and Wicca and the West. It proves that paganism is truly international, no matter what variant it may take in certain localities. There are already dozens of publications for pagans, some reputable, some less so, some impressive, some primitive. A magazine called *The Pagan* is obtainable from Box 2953, St. Louis, Missouri; a newsletter called *The Wiccan*, which calls itself the organ of the pagan front, appears at BM-HcM, Monomark, London WC1, England, and *Waxing Moon*, is obtainable from BCM-Waxing, London, WC1, England. Undoubtedly, other, more ambitious, projects in the publication field will follow.

If there is some question in the minds of scientists who are not theologians as to the validity of orthodox religion, the existence of God and of a hereafter, a somewhat different problem presents itself to the scientifically minded in dealing with pagan realities. Setting aside one's emotional involvement for the moment, a logical and scientifically minded person must eventually ask himself: Are there deities? Is there a Diana somewhere out there? If one invokes the gods, can they hear one and do they really come to one's aid? As far as the Masters are concerned, this problem does not prevent itself to such an extent since the Masters apparently are human beings who have passed on and are now existing in the next dimension. Thus, the question of the Masters' reality is closely related to the problem of survival of human personality with which I have dealt extensively in *Life After Death: The Challenge and the Evidence.*

Certainly, if ordinary people can continue to exist beyond physical death, then extraordinary individuals possessed of great wisdom and power can do so to an even greater degree. But what about the deities, those who were never of human status? Are they figments of the imagination created by man to have recourse to in times of stress and trouble? Are they abstractions? Are they symbolic projections from one's own self given fanciful names to make them more understandable and closer to one's own view of the universe?

I have never met a pagan who subscribes to the three-dimensional belief in the physical presences of the gods the way ordinary people did in ancient Greece and Rome. There the gods were simply people with greater powers, who had all the physical characteristics of humans, but with additional abilities to transcend the limitations imposed upon mortals.

When pagans speak of seeing the goddess in meditation or during a rite, they see her all right. However, the meeting of mortal and goddess occurs on the *inner planes* rather than on the physical level. Sometimes, through astral projection of the inner self, the worshiper encounters thought forms on the inner planes, temporarily lifted outside and above his physical body in ecstasy. Whether through scrying, or ritual, or through meditation, the contact point is always his nonphysical self.

Granted that man can see, hear, or feel the goddess or any

of the other deities of the pantheistic world, the question still
arises whether these gods are individual, clearly defined entities
even if not human, or whether they are exteriorations of the
worshiper's own self. Here we stumble upon the same difficulties we have stumbled on before when trying to pin down the
reality of the God of orthodox religion. We cannot be quite
sure if the gods of the pagans are independent forces in the
universe, as is indeed suggested in some of the foregoing material by those who should know, or whether they are merely
part of the godhead within each of us. Possibly they are both.
One of the attractions of the new pagan movement is the
mystique that still surrounds, and will forever surround, some
of its inner teachings. It really doesn't matter whether a worshiper evokes Diana and visualizes her as an independent goddess
with powers of her own to grant or refuse, or whether, in invoking Diana, he is merely calling upon certain aspects of his own
personality which he thus channels and draws out of himself to
serve him for a particular purpose. If, without this evocation of
Diana, the purpose has not been fulfilled and if, by invoking the
goddess, it does occur, then magic has taken place. That ultimately is the sole purpose of all religion, especially the pagan
religions.

Although the religious and philosophical aspects of the new
paganism are of great importance and will continue to mystify
the scientifically minded, the theological aspects of paganism
are not the most potent reason for the current revival. In terms
of human development and self-realization, the new pagans are
accomplishing things that are new not only for this generation
and those to come, but may well save this world from total
destruction at its own hands.

If there is ever to be a Pagan Manifesto, it will surely contain
these clauses, to which pagans may freely subscribe or not, as
they desire:

1. Thou shalt always be thyself—saying, thinking, doing, what
thou truly desirest so long as it hurts no one else.

2. Thou shalt live in accordance with the laws of nature, not against it, and coordinate sleep, food, physical exertion, and work with the ways of nature.

3. Thou shalt not destroy nature or take from it without restoring that which has been taken, and thou shalt keep the balance of nature intact at all times.

4. Thou shalt worship in any way it pleases thee and let others do likewise even though ye may not understand their ways.

5. Thou shalt not take the life of another individual for any cause whatsoever, and thou shalt not kill animals, save for food and when absolutely necessary, and in the most humane manner possible.

6. Thou shalt not cage another human being or free animal.

7. Thou shalt be free to love whomever thou please so long as thy primary obligations to family, home, and community are not neglected.

8. Thou shalt express thyself through art, craft, music, dancing, singing, and poetry, for in so doing, thou shalt come closer to the rhythm of nature.

9. Thou shalt accept as natural communication with those who have gone on and with the world beyond and the inner planes, and thou shalt develop psychic abilities as a natural function of personality, not as an adjunct.

10. Thou shalt always strike a happy balance between mind and body, exercising them both, and develop thy inner self through the interplay of both thy halves, ever mindful that the spirit is above and beyond both mind and body.

11. And thou shalt not forget the spirit within and the spirit without are the one and only true God.